Ragamuffin Too

Ragamuffin Too

Rocked by Grace

RICHARD A. MILLER

RESOURCE *Publications* • Eugene, Oregon

RAGAMUFFIN TOO
Rocked by Grace

Resource Publications
An Imprint of Wipf and Stock Publishers
199 W. 8th Ave., Suite 3
Eugene, OR 97401

www.wipfandstock.com

PAPERBACK ISBN: 978-1-6667-6403-1
HARDCOVER ISBN: 978-1-6667-6404-8
EBOOK ISBN: 978-1-6667-6405-5

05/01/23

Contents

Permissions

Abbreviations

ESV = English Standard Version: 500 verses allowed

ERV = Easy to read version: 1000 verses allowed

HCSB = Holman Christian Standard Bible: 250 verses allowed

KJV = King James Version: Public domain: 500 verses in the UK

NASB = New American Standard Bible: 1000 verses allowed

NKJV = New King James Version: 500 verses allowed

NIV = New International Version: 500 verses allowed

NLT = New Living Translation: 500 verses allowed

TLB = The Living Bible = TLB: up to 500 verses allowed

Chapter 1

Beginnings

"We should be astonished at the goodness of God, stunned that He should bother to call us by name, our mouths wide open at His love, bewildered that at this very moment we are standing on holy ground."

BRENNAN MANNING, *THE RAGAMUFFIN GOSPEL*[1]

I WAS NOT NEW to Christianity when I first picked up *The Ragamuffin Gospel* by Brennan Manning nearly two decades ago. However, my understanding of Christianity was more along the lines of "sinners in the hands of an angry God." Therefore, it was both joy and relief to learn that while God was indeed perfect and holy, He was also love and grace.

I thank Brennan for making that introduction, as it proved to be a turning point in my life. While this book may be viewed as another chapter in the ongoing saga of fellow Ragamuffin's, it is also a record of my gospel journey over the last twenty years. With that as a launch point, I will share with you not only my victories

1. Manning, *Ragamuffin Gospel*.

and failures, but my personal discoveries and "Aha moments!" along the way.

I hope that not only will you experience the furious love of God spoken so eloquently by Manning, but that you will be challenged to step into your new identity as a beloved child of the Master of the universe and His Son, Jesus. As part of that transformation process, I hope you will also experience the call that God has on your life as you discover the passions that He has built into your very DNA since the beginning of time, as well as the purpose He has for your life. Finally, and perhaps most importantly, I pray that you will discover the divine power source available to all who believe. May that power source give you all you need to uncover and live out the glorious plan that God has for your life in the building of His kingdom.

If you picked up this book knowing that you already have all the answers about God you need, you should stop here. This book is not intended for Christians who already have all the answers. It is not a pep rally to cheer on those who need to be applauded for their spiritual accomplishments or who are looking for a pat on the back for getting a perfect score on their own religious SAT exam.

It is not for people looking for an audience to affirm their spiritual conquests. It is not for those seeking some shrouded mystery that they can continue to guard with the satisfaction that they know something the rest of the world does not.

It is not for those who have it all figured out or those who are content to simply accumulate knowledge rather than risk putting the words of Jesus to work in a world desperate to find the truth.

So, who is this book for?

It is for those who wish to intimately know a God who is not always safe or predictable, but who is always good.

It is for those who are honest enough with themselves to know they don't have all the answers but who hunger and thirst for the knowledge of a God who is goodness and love.

It is for those who are ready to receive the gift of God's unmerited grace and favor without doing anything to qualify for His gift.

It is for those who are ready to accept their place in the family of God and who are thirsty to understand more about the identity of being loved, forgiven, called, and empowered by God to be agents of change in a lost and needy world.

It is for anyone who longs to hear the still small voice of God calling them further. Calling them into an adventure that is not always easy, not always convenient, and not always painless or trouble-free, but is an adventure that brings challenge, change, and joy that continues for eternity.

Finally, I wrote this for myself and anyone else who is curious enough to discover more about their place at the table of the Father who is infinite, eternal, unchangeable, and who is the very definition of love.—Richard Miller

REFLECTIONS OF AN AGING PRINCE

It may seem arrogant to some that I refer to myself as a prince, but in reality, it is just the opposite. It has taken 50 years of my life to get to a place where I can accept that I am a valued, respected, and forgiven member of God's royal family. I spent far too much time running and hiding from a God that I knew I had offended. Fortunately for me (and you too), Jesus paid it all. In this context and with vast gratitude, I share these moments, these lessons learned, with you.

It is my hope that these insights will faithfully reflect my journey from a homeless vagabond to a royal family member. These personal experiences and insights are a part of my story, and I share them with you not as a textbook on how to live the Christian life, not as a theological treatise about how I arrived at all the right answers, and not as a how-to-guide to a life of spiritual superiority. I share my story because I believe that humans innately understand that they are a part of a larger story—God's story. God reveals His heart, His mind, and His purpose as He plays out His story in the lives of those who have gone before and continues to reveal Himself in our stories.

In my story.

In your story.

God in Christ is here with us, between the lines of each event, each disaster and triumph. And He loves us more than we will ever be able to comprehend.

> *If I ascend into heaven, You are there;*
> *If I make my bed in hell, behold, You are there.*
> -Psalm 139:8 KJV

This journey is all about seeing. Until you see yourself as fearfully and wonderfully made and tragically and fatally flawed, you will never understand the world in which you live or your place in it.

You must have a new pair of eyes for this seeing to happen. You must learn to see differently. You must get a fresh perspective and see from a different angle.

But it is not as simple as turning the book upside down or squinting your eyes or putting on a pair of 3-D glasses. This new way of seeing, this new vision, comes only as a gift. It can only be given and can only be received.

It runs contrary to common wisdom that "you get what you pay for" because you can't pay for this gift, no matter how rich you are. It comes freely and yet has a value above anything else in the world. It defies the "protestant work ethic" and the "self-made man theory," both of which state that if you work hard, apply yourself, study diligently and ponder deeply, then you can uncover the deep mysteries of the universe.

You can't uncover this mystery. It must be revealed to you.

As an example, let me point you to the most successful failure in history: Christopher Columbus. Columbus had a vision of what could be—he had a conviction, not just that the world was round, but that he, Christopher Columbus, was destined to be THE ONE to discover the circular, all-water route from Europe to India. He was obsessed with the idea and convinced of his ability to complete the task. Columbus allowed no obstacle to stand in his way. He persevered for years in the quest for venture capital.

He even changed his citizenship to get what he needed. History records Christopher Columbus as one of the greatest explorers of all time. He is credited with making one of the most significant discoveries of his millennium.

For Europeans, he did reveal a whole New World. He explored extensively, collected evidence, made public his findings, and launched a new age in the history of western civilization. Yet, technically, he was a failure. He did not find an all-water route to the riches of the Far East. He did not open up a new trade route with India. So, Columbus went to his grave, convinced he had accomplished something that he had not.

The point is that he couldn't see the truth because it did not fit his narrative of how his life should go. For each of us to discern the truth, we must see the world with a Holy Spirit-informed eyesight. Then, and only then, will we perceive the universe as it truly is. And when we do, our lives will be forever changed. As Jesus said,

Then you will know the truth and the truth will set you free.
– John 8:32

Are you free?
Really free?

WATCH NIGHT

Imagine the evening of December 31, 1863, just hours before the Emancipation Proclamation, which had been announced by Abraham Lincoln more than a year before, was scheduled to go into effect. If you were a slave in America, what must it have been like to watch the clock slowly tick toward midnight?

That evening was so powerful that it has been forever woven into the fabric of many African American churches. Today, it continues to be celebrated as a Watch Night Service on New Year's Eve.

As the clock strikes midnight, it is complete. The Executive Order has been issued. It is now law.

One second you are a slave and the next, you are free.

Not potentially free, but actually free.

Not temporarily free, but permanently free.

Not just free in theory or free in mind, but free in body and in spirit— free indeed.

Absolutely free.

No longer restrained by the laws and customs of the past. No longer identified as the property of another. No longer forced to do the will of someone else. You have been set free!

> *Free at last, Free at last, Praise God Almighty, we are free at last.*
> –Martin Luther King, Jr.[2]

So how about you? Has the truth set you free?

---

2. King, "I Have a Dream Speech."

Chapter 2

The Rest of the Story

"Do you believe that the God of Jesus loves you beyond worthiness and unworthiness, beyond fidelity and infidelity-that He loves you in the morning sun and in the evening rain-that He loves you when your intellect denies it, your emotions refuse it, your whole being rejects it? Do you believe that God loves without condition or reservation and loves you this moment as you are and not as you should be?"

BRENNAN MANNING[1]

I HAVE BEEN A Christian for nearly 40 years and a dad for more than 30 of those years. I have been a father to four exceptional biological children, and a teacher, father figure, coach and mentor to thousands of others who were my students or players at one time or another.

I wish that I could say I have represented our faith and our God honestly, faithfully, and compassionately to all of them all the time. I could say it, but they would know the truth, even if the rest

---

1. Manning and Blasé, *All Is Grace.*

of the reading public did not. They would know that I have loved them well at times, and at others, I have failed miserably.

For the times that you have allowed me to share your lives, your trials, and your triumphs, I wish to express my deepest gratitude to my children, players, and students. Those shared experiences have been some of the most memorable and meaningful moments of my life. Thank you.

For all those times I have failed you, I beg your forgiveness. I make no excuses for my shortcomings. When I have been impatient and short-tempered, it was because I wasn't getting my way. When I told you one thing and then did another, it was because I am a flawed human being intent on seeking my own selfish interests. I cannot go back in time and fix my mistakes, but there is One who has atoned for all my missteps, mishaps, and miscues, and that is what this story is about.

THE REST OF THE STORY

I am convinced that the message of the Gospel is much greater than you may have been led to believe. What is standard fare in the institutional church is the desire to calculate, quantify, and regulate the religious system. In that way, with a series of checklists, rules, and regulations, we can measure our progress and compare how we are doing to everyone else.

Hidden within this worldview are twin agendas. First, the creation of a religious class system: the upper-class is for those who keep the rules and complete the checklists while the lower-class refers to those who fail to keep the rules and complete the tasks as required. Second, controlling the Creator. If, after all, we keep the rules and complete the lists, if we do more good deeds than evil, then surely this creator God must be obligated, according to our system, to reward us. Right?

Hmmm, maybe not.

What if. . .?

The American church tends to ask, "What? What is God? What do I have to do to be on His good side? What is my punishment or what is my reward?"

I want to challenge you to ask, "What if. . .?"

What if there is someone who loves you more perfectly than you have ever known? Someone, not an impersonal cosmic force, but a person, a being, who loves you enough to pursue you through all your toxic mistakes and missteps? Someone who cares enough to rescue you from this mess and someone who loves you as you are, not as you should be?

What if the reality of life is that we are infinitely valued and cherished by God?

What if the reality is that we can experience the overwhelming love of God now, instead of after we are dead?

What if, in reality, God has already done everything required for you to live a life of purpose and spend eternity with Him?

What if death and pain and suffering were not the ultimate evil?

What if you were rich beyond measure right now and didn't even know it?

What if life was a gift to be enjoyed and not a trial to be survived?

What if Jesus operated in this world, seeking only synchronicity with His Father, and thereby disabled or marginalized the opinions of the religious powerbrokers of His day?

What if salvation is more than just gratitude? What if it is "Ah-ha!" Discovery? Revelation? Epiphany?

What if it is a new vision with new eyes?

What if there is one truth so profound, so compelling that it changes everything—every human construct and every established human understanding?

A journey of a thousand miles begins with just one step.
– Lao Tzu[2]

---

2. Lao Tzu, "Chapter 64."

Let's journey together as we seek to find what King Solomon said was more important than silver and gold. So important, in fact, that he challenges us to discover it, even if it costs us all we have.

What is this treasure?

Wisdom.

Wisdom is the most precious of all possessions. Where does wisdom come from and how can we acquire it?

When I was a young man, I was determined to do things my way, to take on any and every obstacle and overcome it on my terms.

Honestly, that is a painful way to live and an expensive way to operate. The pain was literal—broken bones, stitches, and scars remind me of the cost to this day. One thing is for sure, scars are souvenirs that last a lifetime.

Slowly, I began to understand that the older people in my life had knowledge and understanding that could help me make better decisions. Why? Because they had lived life for 50 years longer than me and had made their own mistakes and lived with the consequences of their own choices, both good and bad. And they were more than willing to share their insights if I would but ask.

I learned to ask.

But, in addition to life experience, wisdom is a capacity of the mind that allows us to perceive life from God's perspective, discernment that comes from the spiritual dimension.

In Proverbs, Solomon encourages us to "get wisdom."

> *Those who get wisdom, love life; That it's better to get wisdom than gold and that those who get wisdom, find life and receive favor from the Lord.* –Proverbs 19:8 NIV

So, as we begin this journey together, I encourage you to seek after God's wisdom. You won't be sorry.

But wisdom won't come easy. So, what is wisdom?

Simply stated, while knowledge is truth about things, wisdom is using truth to make honest and appropriate decisions in a timely manner. Wisdom is more than just knowing the truth; it is using truth to act properly at just the right time for the right reason.

My personal experience tells me that wisdom is the most sacred of formulas, an amalgam of knowledge and experience, forged in the fires of adversity that lays dormant until activated by the breath of the Spirit. It remains a mere speck of latent potential, unrealized until buried in the fertile soil of brokenness, watered by the tears of humility and warmed by the gentle, insistent rays of grace, finally to be awakened from sleep by the still small voice of God.

Chapter 3

The Gift

A trusting heart is forgiven, and in turn, forgives."
BRENNAN MANNING, *ALL IS GRACE*[1]

COMPETE OR COMPLETE? STRIVE or thrive? What drives you?

The movie *Chariots of Fire* was released in 1980. The film is based on two elite runners who competed in the 1924 Olympics— Harold Abrahams and Eric Liddell. Abrahams represented Great Britain, and Liddell competed for his home country, Scotland. Competing for their countries was both an honor and a weighty responsibility.

Abrahams loved the thrill of victory and was proud to represent his nation. But, like many top athletes today, he was also obsessed with winning. So, he held nothing back, and the 1924 Olympics gave him a goal to aim for and an outlet for his passion: winning.

Eric Liddell was a rugby player, a sprinter, and a missionary to China. He was devout in his commitment to God. That commitment caused him to refuse to run in the 100-meter sprint, which

1. Manning and Blasé, *All Is Grace*.

was his strongest event, because the race was to be run on a Sunday. Instead, he chose to honor God's direction to rest on the Sabbath, and as a result, he forfeited the opportunity to run the race he had the best chance of winning. But his story did not end there. Liddell chose instead to compete in the 400-meter sprint that was to be run on a weekday. The result? He won a gold medal in that event and set a new world record. After the Olympics, he returned to China to serve as a teacher and missionary, where he remained until his death at the age of 43 in a Japanese internment camp.

While the two men were both superior athletes and competed in the same arena, they operated with distinctly different motivations. In the film, Abrahams says, "And now, in one hour's time, I will be out there again. I will raise my eyes and look down that corridor, four feet wide, with ten lonely seconds to justify my whole existence. But will I?"

Liddell saw things from a different perspective. "I believe God made me for a purpose, but He also made me fast, and when I run, I feel His pleasure."

Tim Keller shares this insight in his book *The King's Cross*: "Harold Abrahams was weary even when he rested, and Eric Liddell was rested even when he was exerting himself. Why? Because there's a work underneath our work that we really need rest from. It's the work of self-justification."[2]

Call it what you will, but the burden of trying to prove your worth to a watching world is a losing proposition because enough will never be enough.

> *Hell and destruction are never full; so the eyes of man are never satisfied*—Proverbs 27:20 KJV

In the same way that Hell always has room for one more soul, our desires and our constant need for recognition are never fully gratified. Only God can satisfy our need for significance. When we put our confidence in Him, then everything changes.

2. Keller, *King's Cross*.

But those who trust in the Lord will find new strength. They will soar high on wings like eagles. They will run and not grow weary. They will walk and not faint. -Isaiah 40:31 NLT

Like Abrahams, I know what it means to be driven. Driven to compete. Driven to win. Driven to prove. But I'm trying to course correct.

When I was younger, I had a really hard time walking away from any challenge no matter how extreme. One of them could have cost me my life.

The challenge? Ride my bike across America, from Virginia to California. When I use the word bike, I'm referring to a bicycle not a motorcycle. Friends suggested that it was impossible, but I was in my twenties, the age of invincibility.

What would it mean? Riding a bicycle across the entire width of the United States, a distance of 2200 miles in less than 30 days. I would begin in the mountains of Virginia, wind through Tennessee, cross the swampy lowlands of Mississippi and Arkansas, endure across Oklahoma, and ascend the Rocky Mountains, first climbing 7,700 feet to the Clines Corner crossing and then descending over 7,000 feet into Albuquerque, New Mexico. The ride up the Rocky Mountains? *Grueling* is the word, and down the other side was *hair raising*. Our speedometers topped out at 50 miles per hour and all we could do was hang on for dear life. From New Mexico, we still had to cross the Mojave Desert in July at a temperature of 112 degrees. As we crossed into Arizona, I crashed, bad enough to make a trip to the ER. Two black eyes, twenty-one stitches over my right eye, and road rash up and down my side. Later that day, I tapped into the last reserves of energy that I could muster, and we kept moving west. We had planned to ride the final 167 miles from Flagstaff to Kingman, Arizona in two days, but after my crash we decided to ride the entire distance in a single day because with my right eye nearly swollen shut, I feared both of my eyes would be compromised if we delayed. Old war pilots used the phrase "coming in on a wing and prayer" to describe harrowing returns after a mission. That's how I rode the last leg. The next day, we finally crossed the Colorado River into California.

Mission complete. 2200 miles in twenty-one days. Stupid. Driven. And unforgettable.

Now, decades later, a little older and a little wiser, I find joy and satisfaction in the knowledge that God takes pleasure when I run; that is, when I do what I was created for.

> *Come to me, all you who are weary and burdened, and I will give you rest. Take my yoke upon you and learn from me, for I am gentle and humble in heart, and you will find rest for your souls. For my yoke is easy and my burden is light.* -Matthew 11:28 NIV

At the end of the day, it's your race to run. No one else can do it for you. But remember this, while only you can run your race, God takes great pleasure when He sees you drop every weight and run!

When we rest in the confidence of God's love, we find that He is gentle and kind in spirit. He promises to give us rest and as we accept His teaching, the load He gives us to carry is light.

So, what now?

Dive headfirst into your passions! Discover all the gifts you've been given. Don't think twice, don't look back, don't ask why me? Instead, ask, what's next? Rest in the knowledge that God in Christ is with you in every moment of joy and pain, that He alone knows what is best for you.

> *Commit your way to the Lord; trust in him, and he will act.*
> -Psalm 37:5 ESV

One final anecdote. As Eric Liddell was warming up for his historic run, he was handed a folded note by one of the team trainers; it read, "The old book says, 'He that honors me, I will honor.'" A reference to 1 Samuel 2:30. Liddell was deeply moved and I'm sure that it confirmed his belief that God took great pleasure when he ran.

> *I keep my eyes always on the Lord.*
> *With him at my right hand, I will not be shaken.*
> *You make known to me the path of life,*
> *you will fill me with joy in your presence,*
> *with eternal pleasures at your right hand.*
> -Psalm 16:8 NIV

THE GIFT

A few years back, I wrote a letter to my grown children. I'd like to share it with you here as I believe it will provide a context for understanding a father's perspective.

A Message from your Dad

I have realized that it's hard to find a gift that is "one size fits all" in today's world. What can I possibly give you that you don't already have? You all have jobs, families, some money saved, and are relatively self-sufficient. Perhaps, there is nothing I can give you that you don't already possess. But maybe, like the Wizard of Oz, I can make you aware of how rich you already are.

Let me begin by giving you your freedom. You may be thinking, "Thanks, but I already have it. I'm on my own; I have a job, I have a car, I already have everything I need."

But, if you read carefully, what you discover may save you from years of frustration.

I want to free you from what I call the "burden of proof."

The first time I got hit by a car, I was 10 years old, and it was all my brother's fault. He thought he was "top dog" and always tried to keep me in my place.

The year was 1966, and we had just moved from the mountains of Virginia to the San Francisco suburb of Palo Alto, California. Among the discoveries we made in our early explorations of this new locale was a place called 7-Eleven, and a concoction known as a Slurpee. I know that Slurpee's seem like an everyday part of life, but they were unique and incredible back in the day!

After an afternoon stop at 7-Eleven, as we were finishing our frozen delights, your uncle issued a challenge that would nearly cost me my life.

"I'll race you home!"

Now to some people, that might not sound like much, but to a younger brother, it was an inescapable challenge. So, like a moth drawn to a flame, the younger brother is not allowed to dodge a dare issued by the elder (I think that's the 11th commandment).

Now, I wouldn't want to prejudice you, but there are some facts that you need to know ahead of time to fully appreciate the monumental task ahead of me.

The 7-Eleven in question was located five blocks from home, and my brother had a faster bike than I did. He was also two and a half years older and. . .

He was known to cheat.

If I was going to win, I would have to outthink him and out-ride him!

Another important factor is knowing that my brother was the cautious one by nature while I. . . I was something other than that.

Even at 10-years-old, I was enough of a psychologist to know that this lack of caution was my sole advantage.

I also knew that one block from our house was a busy inter-section with a stop sign facing our direction. As we put the first few blocks of the race behind us, he slowly began to pull ahead of me. But as we neared the final stretch, I still had my "ace in the hole."

I knew that he would do something foolish when he came to the intersection with the stop sign.

He would stop.

And this would be all the edge I needed!

Sure enough, as we approached the intersection at breakneck speed, even though he was leading by several bike lengths, he be-gan to slow down, and that's when I made my move!

I blew by him like Tony Stewart passing Rusty Wallace on the outside of turn four. He was at a dead stop, and I was at full speed!

As I flew by, with the wind in my hair and a smile on my face, I knew I had won!!!

It was glorious!

For about a second and a half.

I don't know if it was the sound of the car tires screeching or the sensation of being catapulted across the street and into the hedge that got my attention first. Still, in that brief moment, the thrill of victory melted into the agony of defeat.

Now, before you get too worried, I didn't die. The damage wasn't severe. The agony lay not in my injuries but in knowing that I had failed. The driver of the car was upset and frantic. Along with my brother, the motorist came over to check on me and what remained of my bike. My brother, all the while, feigned concern about my well-being.

But I knew, we both knew, that he was inwardly gloating.

First, my bike was a total loss.

Second, we knew I was really going to get it when I got home. And finally,

He knew that he had won.

So, what's my point?

It is simple. Some of us—whether 10-years-old, 21-years-old, or 60-years-old—live with a chip on our shoulder.

We are born to compete, to strain, and to strive. We carry a burden—a need to be better, stronger, faster, smarter, cooler, whatever. We live our lives like we have something to prove.

And even when it comes to heaven, we feel as though we must earn God's love.

I call this the *burden of proof.*

As my first gift to you, I'm going to let you in on a secret. The contest to be on top or the competition to be number one, is a battle you can't win.

Enough is never enough.

There will always be someone better, faster, stronger or more intelligent. But even if you somehow make it to the top, above all other competition, there are two inescapable facts that you must know:

At the top:

- You are alone

- The stay is only temporary

So, what am I saying?
Don't try?

Settle for a mediocre life?

Live with Mom and Dad for the next 30 years?

None of the above.

Simply this: You can't do enough, have enough, or be enough to fill the hole in your life that needs filling.

You can't earn God's love.

There is nothing you can do that will make Him love you more, and there is nothing you can do to make Him love you less. So, hear this; as a son of Adam, you can't measure up, but as a child of God, you already have.

You are loved.

You are forgiven.

God said it, so that settles it.

Now, once you know that simple truth, you can begin to play the game by a whole different set of rules.

I am nothing but He is everything.

I can't do it alone, but with Him, nothing is impossible.

When I seek Him first, everything else is mine.

If and when you can accept that you have nothing to prove, you are suddenly free to discover rather than compete.

You are free to give rather than get.

You are free to accept rather than earn God's love.

The martyred missionary Jim Elliot said it best: *"He is no fool who gives away what he cannot keep, to gain what he cannot lose."*[3]

When you give it all up, you get it all back.

Set the burden of proof aside and live each day as a gift.

The second important thing I want you to know is love:

An ancient Greek philosopher said, *"One word frees us of all the weight and pain of life: that word is love."*[4]

Victor Hugo captures the importance of love when he wrote, *"To love another person is to see the face of God."*[5]

And the Apostle Paul said it:

---

3. Elliot, *Journals of Jim Elliot*.

4. Sophocles, *Antigone*.

5. Hugo, *Les Miserables*.

*"Though I speak with the voice of men and of angels, if
I have not love, I am a noisy gong or clanging cymbal"*
-1 Corinthians 13:1 ESV

I hope you realize just how much you are loved, not because of what you have achieved, your good looks, or because you are funny.

I love you because you are mine.

Guess what? The same is true with God. He loves you because you are His.

When I consider the absolute essentials that I want you to know, it comes down to just two things:

I want you to be free. And I want to be sure that you know that you are loved.

I love you.

Your Mom loves you. And God loves you.

Over the years, I have seen delightful layers of each of you revealed. I have been intrigued by your insights, amused by your imperfections, and irritated by your impertinence.

As an imperfect father, I assure you that if I can love you then God, your Heavenly Father, loves you even more.

Being confident of this love, both His and ours, will empower you to live with confidence, enthusiasm, and compassion, never settling for second best.

To live a life uncommon.

I have a dream, and in that dream, I see my children.

I see you, free from fear and armed with love. You have become our messengers to the world and to the future.

Free from guilt and armed with love, yours are the voices that intercede for those who have no voice.

Free from greed and armed with love, yours are the hands that reach out to feed the hungry.

Free from pressure and armed with love, yours become the arms that embrace the widows and orphans of the world.

Free to hope and armed with love, yours are the feet that carry the message of God's love to the far corners of the world.

Free to dream and armed with love, you are instruments in the hands of God Almighty to preserve, redeem, and transform this dark world into His kingdom of light.

You are our messengers to the world and to the future.

Be free. Be loved. Live in peace.

All my love,

Dad

Chapter 4

Big Lies

"My deepest awareness of myself is that I am deeply loved by Jesus Christ and I have done nothing to earn it or deserve it."

BRENNAN MANNING[1]

THE TRUTH VS THE LIE

LUCIFER. STAR OF THE morning. Angel of Light. Heaven's most beautiful angel. And the world's greatest liar.

In this age of science and technology, we have knowledge and information at our fingertips. New innovations and discoveries are made every day, so it is easy to dismiss the reality of the spirit world.

Because we can't see either angels or demons and can't use science to prove the existence of God and Satan, the temptation is to relegate matters of the spirit to the category of myths, legends, and fairytales. We do so at our own peril.

1. Manning, *Ragamuffin Gospel.*

Often, in modern society, we live exclusively according to the "rules of evidence" established by the scientific community. In our culture, if we can't see it, taste it, feel it or reproduce it in a laboratory, then it isn't real.

Lucifer has had thousands of years to perfect his craft of deceit. To practice the art of bait and switch. He intimately understands the nature of man and has mastered the art of mixing a lot of truth with a little bit of falsehood to poison our thinking about God.

He started it with Eve:

> *"You will not certainly die," the serpent said to the woman, "For God knows that when you eat from it your eyes will be opened, and you will be like God, knowing good and evil."*-Genesis 3:5 HCSB

He started with Eve and has been hard at work ever since to cause us to question the character of God.

Over the course of human history, The Great Liar has refined two primary lies that feed upon the weaknesses of man. If the first one doesn't work, the second one often will.

The first one goes something like this:

> *"Because of your sins, missteps, and mistakes, you are worthless, and God is angry with you. He is so angry, and you are so debased that you deserve both punishment in this life and consignment to hell in the next one."*

He makes sure to remind you every day just what a loser you are. Each time you fail to live up to your inner conscience, he repeats the lie of your worthlessness and reminds you that God has no time for someone like you. In fact, he is incensed at your behaviors and is lining up punishments just for you.

DARK SIDE OF THE SOUL

"I talk with You every day expectantly, hoping to hear Your voice, but the only sound I hear is the rattle and din of the chains of my fundamental slavery.

Daily, I implore others to believe in Your unconditional, unqualified, unwarranted love for them while feeling myself to be unworthy, unqualified, and unfit.

Awash in a sea of evidence that testifies to Your love for all of humanity, I am deaf to the sound of the still, small voice that whispers Your words of love to me."

I recently came across this entry that I had written in one of my journals some time back. I remember the solitude and darkness that draped itself like a shroud around my being. As I reflect now upon my condition, I realize that the hopelessness that darkened my soul that day was, to a degree, self-induced or self-inflicted. Yes, the Father of Lies enhanced the darkness, but often I chose to believe what he said about me. I write of it now to remind myself, and as a service to anyone who needs to see some light at the end of the tunnel.

What I finally discovered was this. When I choose to pursue my desires exclusively and chart my own destination, sin's false promises of freedom become a terrifying weapon in the arsenal of Satan. I can become so preoccupied with pursuing my personal agenda, chasing my dreams, and indulging my appetites that I can't hear the voice of God. I begin to forget both my identity and the purpose of my life.

But wait, it gets worse.

Once "done" with sin's false promises of freedom, I tend to get overwhelmed with feelings of guilt and shame. I am once again deaf to the quiet voice of a loving Savior as He speaks words of love, forgiveness, redemption, rescue, and sonship into my heart.

It happens then only occasionally, when I find myself between the peak of self-indulgence and the dark valley of defeat, that I am in a state of being where I can hear His voice.

While I linger in this place long enough to be reminded of His love, that state of heart and soul cannot hold its own against the ever-present voices of darkness. So, once again, I slowly but surely become deaf to the voice of God.

There are temporary respites on the tableland between the peaks of self-importance and the slough of despondency. Interludes where I am not preoccupied with the voyeuristic adrenaline of my sin or the debilitating noise of my shame. It is in these quiet spaces I remember the echoes of peace and joy and hope and love that I fleetingly hear between my two conditions; it is here that I choose obedience.

Yes, obedience.

I choose obedience over the fraudulent promises of freedom presented by the dark side so that I might stay in this place of confidence and rest.

It is in obedience that I find the peace and contentment, love and joy, satisfaction and comfort that I have searched for all of my life. I pray that I might remain here to experience the joy that is a fundamental benefit of a relationship with our Father and His Son and the Spirit that indwells each of His children.

The choice becomes rather simple: false freedom promised by the dark side or tangible joy that comes from hearing His voice and realizing His love.

I choose obedience, and I find joy.

THAT OLD-TIME RELIGION AND TWO BIG LIES

I grew up in a religion with endless prohibitions and demands. It was rooted fully in a particular worldview: the depravity of man, the surety of damnation, and a fiery hell for sinners and anyone who hung out with them. God is in His heaven, constantly watching with a critical eye, keeping record of each sin and misstep. Divine punishment was never far from our minds and there were carefully chosen Bible verses to support our paranoia.

What those religionists were trying to sell me was a view that being a Christian is somehow connected to keeping a list of rules and regulations, and that God is much like a grumpy, if not angry old man: "Cut your hair, shine your shoes, don't go to movies, don't dance and don't listen to rock and roll music."

They used selected verses to communicate God's justice and wrath. For example, God is angry with wicked people and since you have sinned, He is angry with you (Psalm 7:11). Or, God won't hear the prayers of wicked people and because you've transgressed, He does not hear your prayers (Psalm 66:18). They also preached a type of religious Karma—what goes around comes around and you've done some bad things, so punishment is coming your way. Look out!

Tertullian, a Christian that lived early in the Christian era, tells us that in the same way that Christ was crucified between two thieves, there are two thieves that want to steal the good news of the gospel— legalism and license. In this metaphor, the first thief is a legalistic, empty religion comprised of lists of do's and don'ts we must follow as proof to God of how good we are. License is the thief on the other side, communicating that because God loves us, we can do anything we want or make up our own rules of right and wrong with no fear of punishment or consequence.

Both of those views grossly miss the mark. While legalism preaches truth without grace, license promotes grace without truth. Jesus, however, is full of grace and truth. While we have been freed from legalist theology, we have not been left to our own devices or without guidance from God. He is our Father and like any good father He knows that we need direction on how to live a life of purpose and joy. He provides those guidelines in the Bible.

LIE 1: GOD IS ANGRY WITH YOU EVERY DAY

"God is angry with the wicked every day." I was reminded of this often when I was young as an alleged means of curbing my sinful behavior. There is a God, and because He is holy and just, He is offended when we sin. We are "on the outs" with God because of our sin.

Now God might hate the sin and love the sinner, but with a well-oiled precision, the religious aristocracy has managed to blur the line just enough to maintain control over their audience.

To this line of thought, which has etched deep grooves in the collective brains of many of the weary faithful, I want to ask some simple questions:

- Do you have children?
- Do they mess up?
- Do they make mistakes?

My children do. Sometimes I get angry and sometimes I am sad because of the damage they bring upon themselves. But I don't hate my kids. I love them fiercely and absolutely.

In the gospel of Luke, Jesus shares a story with both the lost and miserable and with members of the religious elite, who thought they had it all figured out.

The Parable of the Prodigal Son:

> And He said, "There was a man who had two sons. And the younger of them said to his father, 'Father, give me the share of property that is coming to me. And he divided his property between them. Not many days later, the younger son gathered all he had and took a journey into a far country, and there he squandered his property in reckless living. And when he had spent everything, a severe famine arose in that country, and he began to be in need. So, he went and hired himself out to one of the citizens of that country, who sent him into his fields to feed pigs. And he was longing to be fed with the pods that the pigs ate, and no one gave him anything.
>
> "But when he came to himself, he said, 'How many of my father's hired servants have more than enough bread, but I perish here with hunger! I will arise and go to my father, and I will say to him, "Father, I have sinned against heaven and before you. I am no longer worthy to be called your son. Treat me as one of your hired servants."' And he

arose and came to his father. But while he was still a long way off, his father saw him and felt compassion, and ran and embraced him and kissed him. And the son said to him, 'Father, I have sinned against heaven and before you. I am no longer worthy to be called your son.' But the father said to his servants, 'Bring quickly the best robe, and put it on him, and put a ring on his hand, and shoes on his feet. And bring the fattened calf and kill it and let us eat and celebrate. For this my son was dead, and is alive again; he was lost, and is found.' And they began to celebrate.

"Now, his older son was in the field, and as he came and drew near to the house, he heard music and dancing. He called one of the servants and asked what these things meant. And he said to him, 'Your brother has come, and your father has killed the fattened calf because he has received him back safe and sound.' The son was angry and refused to go in. His father came out and entreated him, but he answered his father, 'Look, these many years I have served you and I never disobeyed your command, yet you never gave me a young goat that I might celebrate with my friends. But when this son of yours came, who has devoured your property with prostitutes, you killed the fattened calf for him!' His father said to him, 'Son, you are always with me, and all that is mine is yours. It was fitting to celebrate and be glad, for this your brother was dead, and is alive; he was lost, and is found.'"—Luke 15:11–32 ESV

So, let me ask, when did the father of the prodigal love his son in this parable? Only after the son had repented and returned home? No, if you read the story carefully, you will see that the father was waiting every day for his son to come home. He saw him "while he was still far off" and ran to meet him. Dig a little deeper and you will see that the father loved his son enough to give him his inheritance early, even though that would have humiliated the father in the culture of his day.

In short, the father always loved his son. Good son, bad son, while he was sinning, when he repented. The father loved his son without reservation or condition.

Brennan Manning puts it this way:

"The gospel of grace announces, forgiveness precedes repentance. The sinner is accepted before he pleads for mercy. It is already granted. He need only receive it. Total amnesty. Gratuitous pardon.

"When the prodigal son limped home from his lengthy binge of waste and wandering, boozing and womanizing, his motives were mixed at best. He said to himself, "How many of my father's hired men have all the food they want and more, and here am I dying of hunger! I will leave this place and go to my father." The ragamuffin's stomach was not churning with compunction because he had broken his father's heart. Disenchanted with life, the wastrel weaved his way home, not from a burning desire to see his father, but just to stay alive.

"For me, the most touching verse in the entire Bible is the father's response: "While he was still a long way off, his father saw him and was moved with pity. He ran to the boy, clasped him in his arms and kissed him." I am moved that the father didn't cross-examine the boy, bully him, lecture him on ingratitude, or insist on any high motivation. He was so overjoyed at the sight of his son that he ignored all the canons of prudence and parental discretion and simply welcomed him home. The father took him back just as he was.

"What a word of encouragement, consolation, and comfort! We don't have to sift our hearts and analyze our intentions before returning home. Abba just wants us to show up. We don't have to tarry at the tavern until purity of heart arrives. We don't have to be shredded with sorrow or crushed with contrition. We don't have to be perfect or even very good before God will accept us. We don't have to wallow in guilt, shame, remorse, and self-condemnation. Even if we still nurse a secret nostalgia for the far country, Abba falls on our neck and kisses us."

Even if we come back to our Father in Heaven because we can't make it on our own, God welcomes us. He will seek no explanations about our sudden appearance.[2]

2. Manning, *Ragamuffin Gospel*.

Did you hear that? God is not angry with us. He is delighted when we come home and wants to celebrate our return. Guess what? My Heavenly Father loves me, and He loves you too. Right here, right now.

As I am, as you are, as we are.

I can almost hear Him saying, *"Come on up to the house!"*

So, did the prodigal son "repent?" Absolutely, but not when or why one might expect. The story clearly tells us that the son decided to return home when he was hungry and broke. He was down and out and needed a job. He went home hoping that his confession would win his father over so that he might at least earn enough to buy some food. He lived with the idea that his sins were so great that his father would not forgive him. Imagine his surprise when his father ran to him and embraced him, even before he was able to blurt out his rehearsed speech of confession!

But it gets better! His father gave him new clothes, shoes, and a ring that indicated he was still an honored member of the family! The younger son wrongly believed that his father was angry with him and would harbor ill will against him because of his reckless behavior. When confronted with the truth of his father's unconditional love, the process of repentance began.

When he came face-to-face with the evidence of his father's great love for a wayward son, it was this truth that set the son free. Praise God!

Repentance has little to do with how sinful you have been. Correctly understood, it is all about how good God is to us! It is just like the God I have come to know. When I was at my worst, God gave me his very best.

> *Or do you presume on the riches of His kindness and for-bearance and patience, not knowing that God's kindness is meant to lead you to repentance?—Romans 2:4 ESV*

LIE 2: I AM THE CENTER OF THE UNIVERSE.

If the Great Liar doesn't hook you with guilt and shame, then he flips the script. He seeks to convince you that you should be the center of the universe and that your needs and wants supersede the concerns of everyone else in the world. You are so special that you deserve anything and everything you want. Just because you have to lie or cheat a little bit to get what you want, it's ok because your desires should come first.

You believe you've worked hard for everything you've got and you deserve to be happy. God helps those who help themselves, right? So, carry on, you deserve to be on top.

In raising this generation of children, I believe we have allowed the pendulum to swing from one side to other. Today, instead of parents being preoccupied with work and social and religious commitments, parents are consumed with making sure their children have every opportunity afforded to them. T-ball, soccer, dance, little league, the list goes on. . . and everyone must get a trophy! The message we are sending to our children is. "*You are the center of the universe. I will drop whatever I am doing to be in attendance at your function.*" (I speak from experience here: I very rarely missed any of children's athletic events, even when it meant traveling across the country to watch them compete.)

Is there a way to love without idolizing? I hope so. It happens when we look at the loved ones in our lives as those born in the image of God, rather than as the center of the universe, that they can truly be loved, and feel supported, cherished, and upheld.

We love our children best when we balance discipline and delight. We delight in their strengths and their passions, but we also hold them to a standard of honesty and respect.

I believe that Jesus lived out that balance. In Matthew chapter 5, He says:

> "*Think not that I am come to destroy the law, or the prophets: I am not come to destroy, but to fulfill. For verily I say unto you, till heaven and earth pass, one jot or one tittle shall in no wise pass from the law, till all be fulfilled.*

Whosoever therefore shall break one of these least com-
mandments, and shall teach men so, he shall be called
the least in the Kingdom of Heaven: but whosoever shall
do and teach them, the same shall be called great in the
Kingdom of Heaven."

The truth that Jesus demonstrated every day is that we are beloved, forgiven, redeemed, equipped, and empowered children of the King. God has rescued us and given us a purpose for our lives. What is that purpose? We are called to work in concert with the Creator, planting the seedlings of faith, hope, and love: a new creation growing toward the Kingdom of Heaven.

Here on earth.

Now.

This is everything, but it might look like nothing. This is joy unceasing, but it may look like dying.

As we sync our lives with the Spirit of God, one day at a time, one decision at a time, one act of love at a time, we are sowing a new reality, seed by seed.

The Kingdom of God is an upside-down kingdom. It beck-
ons us to gamble all, to trust radically, to come and die so
that we might live—to give our lives away. Giving life away
is a paradox. It's losing, so we can win. It's giving so we can
receive. It's risking for security. It's faith. The Kingdom of
God means living that tension."—Ken Wytsma[3]

My daughter spent two years traveling around the world, working with mission groups in 22 different third world countries with an organization called the World Race. She carried all she needed in a backpack and slept wherever there was a place to lie down. Sometimes this was on the floor of a school or church, the roof of a medical clinic, or in a hammock strung between two trees. It was an eye-opening and life changing experience, to say the least. Without a doubt, she was able to see God at work.

On one of the few occasions that we were able to connect with her by phone, she told us about a remarkable experience. Once

3. Wytsma, *Pursuing Justice.*

again, at a mission in the middle of an impoverished country, she and her team were overcome by the poverty in which people lived. Specifically, the children in that village needed, but had no shoes. She and her team of six started their day praying to God, asking for shoes for these children.

Here is an excerpt from her blog:

SHOES FOR THE RACE

It is officially month 6 of the race. Time seems to be speeding by but standing still at the same time. I'm convinced The World Race is a "time warp." Over the last month and a half, a great deal has changed; countries, schedules, food, sleeping arrangements, cultures, and saying goodbye to our amazing alumni squad leaders.

Over the last 5 months, I feel like I have learned and grown more than I could have imagined. I thought to myself, "Okay, I feel good. I've grown enough, my relationship with God has never been stronger and I'm walking in more confidence of who He created me to be. So, what else is there to do these next 5 months on the race?"

Oh man, was there more!! As I've moved from different teams, I've quickly realized the best thing I can do for people is to pray; to surrender things to the Lord and be in continual prayer for my friends, family, and ministry. I don't know why this is something that isn't easier for me to do. Maybe it's the advocate in me or the helper, but if my relationship with the Lord is as strong as I say it is, then I should know God can do far more than I can do.

The practice of continual prayer as a way of life has been transformative. I've seen changes in my family since I've given up "fixing" and replaced it with surrender. I've seen miracles happen when I've stopped doing and started praying.

Just yesterday, the team I am with decided to sit in expectant, big, risky prayer for the ministry we are working with. We prayed that the orphanage we are partnering with can get mattresses for the kids so that they all have beds, and we prayed that the kids would all get shoes so that they wouldn't get any more infections on their feet. We prayed that the lice would go away from their heads, and we prayed for revival in Cambodia.

Hearing these women of God speak things aloud to our Heavenly Father lifted my spirit. It gave me energy and life that I needed as we hit the middle of the race. This race isn't a sprint but a marathon. We are at the point of the race where we are looking down at our feet asking ourselves, "Do I have any more to give?"

After we sat in prayer, I opened my Bible to Luke 10 where I had previously placed a sticky note with a quote. The quote read:

"I stood with my arms outstretched, thanking the Lord for the life that I live. I realized that I was born for a radical life. I was born to set captives free from the bondage of the world. I realized how madly in love I was with the Creator of the world. I realized that my life was Luke 10 and I never wanted it to be any different."

I had read this quote before but this time when I read it, it resonated with me differently. This quote articulates what the race has looked like for us. I now have gotten a glimpse of the phrase in Luke 10: "the harvest is plentiful, but the workers are few."

This race isn't easy, but I can tell you it's worth it.

Only 15 minutes after praying for the needs of those children, we heard the lunch bell ring and we walked over to the kitchen. But in the kitchen, we didn't find lunch. Instead, we found smiling children receiving new sandals for their feet!! Every single one. The joy, smiles and tears experienced in that moment are something I will never forget.

My Father in Heaven knew what these children needed, and He knew what I needed to keep running the race strong.[4]

Enough shoes for all the children in the village.

My daughter and her team were blown away and overwhelmed by the goodness, nearness, and immediacy of God.

When I spoke with her on the phone, she summed it up this way:

4. Miller, "Shoes for the Race."

"Dad, in America, you don't need miracles: you don't believe in miracles because you have money and you have science. But out here, the only hope some of these people have is a miracle, and I have seen with my own eyes—God answers prayers in the most incredible ways."

In America, we don't need miracles.

We don't expect miracles.

We don't see miracles and we miss out on seeing the great God of the universe show up with provision, love, and care.

I am confident of this: God is at work in the world, EVERY SINGLE DAY!

Let's ask Him to give us eyes to see.

We are certainly not designed to be the "center of the universe," but don't be misled. Each of us has a role to play, a destiny to fulfill. A journey to travel and an adventure to enjoy. While we may not be the centerpiece of the puzzle, we are essential to the work of God and His story of rescue, redemption, and the fulfillment of His plan.

Think of a tapestry. If you happen to look at the back of the cloth first, you will see thousands of threads going in multiple directions and angles. It is hard, if not impossible, to envision what the weaver had in mind when he started this piece of woven art. Ahh. . . but when you turn the cloth over! Suddenly, the picture is clear, the story is beautiful!

> For now, we see through a glass, darkly; but then face to
> face: now I know in part; but then shall I know even as
> also I am known.
> - 1 Corinthians 13:12 KJV

That's the way it is with you and me. We are each a small thread in the hands of the Master Weaver! We may not be the center of the universe, but we are essential partners with the Creator. Each thread, each color has a place in the larger picture. Someday, we will see the true masterpiece that He is creating.

The Weaving

My life is but a weaving between my Lord and me,
I cannot choose the colors
He worketh steadily.
Oftimes He weaveth sorrow,
And I in foolish pride
Forget He sees the upper
And I, the underside.
Not till the loom is silent
And the shuttles cease to fly
Shall God unroll the canvas
And explain the reason why.
The dark threads are as needful
In the Weaver's skillful hand
As the threads of gold and silver
In the pattern He has planned.
- Corrie ten Boom[5]

5. ten Boom, *Tramp for the Lord.*

A LETTER FROM JESUS

My child,

I wish that you could see yourself the way that I see you. If you could, you would see how beautiful, how extraordinary you are. If you could, you would see the incredible, talented, creative person that I made you to be; and if you could look into my eyes, you would know beyond any shadow of a doubt that I love you.

You would see in my eyes an absolute knowledge of all that you are without a hint of judgment. You would see welcome and love and delight.

You would see that I don't just "tolerate" you; rather, I delight in you. I celebrate who you are and you would see that together we won't find just temporary happiness; instead, together, we will discover life-long joy.

But I fear that you won't see this about yourself. Instead, you will keep repeating to yourself a story that says, *"I am not lovable, I have messed up, and no one will ever love me. I know what I've done, and my punishment is to live with the shame that comes along with my guilt."*

Satan loves to turn the truth of God into a lie and so, instead of believing that My love is enough, you will go looking for a new story, one that says you can find love and excitement, peace and adventure, gratification and success out there in the world.

And so, you come to fear failure because you believe that success gives you value and worth.

You fear rejection because you look to others and their opinions to validate who you wish you were.

You fear financial loss because you have come to believe that money will bring you peace, safety, and security.

You fear God because you have believed the lie that your value lies in your ability to keep the rules. You assume your worth is based on your performance.

You fear honesty because you can't allow anyone to see behind the curtain.

You fear being nobody because our world tells you that you must be somebody.

Listen to me. Even if you could achieve every success, that would not satisfy what you long for, and you still won't have an answer to your question.

What question you ask?

The only one that matters:

"Am I loved?"

Somewhere out there, along our culture's road to success, fulfillment, love, purpose, acceptance, and approval, you are going to lose something that can't be replaced.

You.

Can you hear me? Can you see what I see? The beautiful you, extraordinary you, the you that I love?

The tragedy is that even if you conquer every army, climb every mountain, and shatter every record in the book, it will not be enough. What good is it if you gain the whole world and lose your own soul? Will you trade what you could be for what the world tells you that you must be?

The truth is that you have nothing to prove and nothing to earn. I've satisfied every condition necessary for you to be forgiven, loved, and complete.

They say that truth is always better than fiction. See that for yourself. That other story, the one that says you aren't enough, will consume you. It will eat you up piece by piece, bit by bit until there is nothing left of you.

But living the truth of who you are and who you were created to be is going to open up a life of possibilities you never dreamed of. It will provide a life that is better than you could have ever imagined.

Satan will keep trying to sell you a cheap imitation of real life. He will sell you instant gratification, satisfaction by hurting others, and getting ahead at all costs. He will sell you an enticing but bankrupt story, and in the end, you'll be left with nothing.

No love.

No joy.

No peace.

No one.

Listen to me! I'm not asking you to give up a life of love and joy and adventure and peace and security. I am asking you to step into it!

With me.

It won't be easy, it won't be comfortable and sometimes it won't be logical, but it will always be good. And day by day, as you get up and show up, and do the best you can to hear my voice and love the people I put in your path, you will begin to see yourself through my eyes. And then,

We'll both dance!

-Jesus[6]

6. By Richard Miller.

Chapter 5

Godisnowhere

"If asked whether I am finally letting God love me, just as I am, I would answer, 'No, but I'm trying.'"

BRENNAN MANNING, *ALL IS GRACE*[1]

CONDITIONAL FORGIVENESS VS ACCOMPLISHED REDEMPTION

EARLIER, I STATED THAT this book is all about seeing—how you see the world, how you see yourself, how you see God.

> *As a man thinketh in his heart, so is he*—King Solomon

How did you read the title of this chapter?
God is nowhere? Or God is now here?
Same letters, same order, entirely different meanings.
A friend once reminded me: "*Perception is everything. Perception is reality until you change the perception.*"

---

1. Manning and Blasé, *All Is Grace*.

Often, when speaking, a different message can be relayed using exactly the same words by putting emphasis on a different word in the sentence. For example:

"I never said she stole my money."

What message do you hear?

Let's go through the sentence by changing the emphasis each time to a different word in the sentence:

I never said she stole my money.

I **never** said she stole my money.

I never **said** she stole my money.

I never said **she** stole my money.

I never said she **stole** my money.

I never said she stole **my** money.

I never said she stole my **money**.

Same sentence. Same exact words. Seven different meanings.

Conditional forgiveness: We are forgiven because Jesus died for us. But. . .. there is always a catch.

Stories are powerful. They directly influence what we believe about the world; that's why it's so important that we tell God's story as accurately as possible. We see the first false storyteller in the Garden of Eden. The serpent told Eve a different story and in doing so, questioned the character of God.

> Genesis 3:1–6 NIV *"Now the serpent was more crafty than any of the wild animals the Lord God had made.*
>
> *He said to the woman, "Did God really say, 'You must not eat from any tree in the garden'?"*
>
> *The woman said to the serpent, "We may eat fruit from the trees in the garden, but God did say, 'You must not eat fruit from the tree that is in the middle of the garden, and you must not touch it, or you will die."*
>
> *"You will not certainly die." the serpent said to the woman. "For God knows that when you eat from it, your eyes will be opened, and you will be like God, knowing good and evil."*
>
> *When the woman saw that the fruit of the tree was good for food and pleasing to the eye, and also desirable*

*for gaining wisdom, she took some and ate it. She also gave
some to her husband, who was with her and he ate it.*

With the help of the Great Liar, she began to question the character of God.

We have been questioning ever since.

Our stories about how the world works create belief systems that obscure, distort, and transpose what we believe about the very nature of God. The story that our culture tells us distracts us with things that don't ultimately matter. As we run after the American Dream, and our sense of individualism or our own self-righteousness, we take lies that are dressed up like the truth and distort our view of the character of God.

The institutional church can tell bad stories too. They can handpick verses from the Bible and explain them to mean something that was not intended by the author. And maybe, because of our background or context, we just hear the words differently, shaped by our worldview and our view of self.

"We hear not as they are but as we are."

For some of us, we then begin to believe that we are worthless and hopeless, as guilty sinners and that God is perpetually angry with us and that punishment lies in wait.

Religious bureaucrats take the love story or our Great Prince and alter it just slightly to make it fit their agenda. Boiled down, their spin is this: We are forgiven if we confess, repent and ask Jesus into our hearts . . . AND

- Go to the front of the church when there's an altar call
- Grovel and beg for His forgiveness or do penance to make up for my mistakes
- Attend an approved church service each and every Sunday
- Memorize lots of Bible verses, don't smoke, don't drink and don't listen to the devil's music

. . . and the list goes on.

There should be a period after the word forgiven. Why? Because Jesus paid the price for my sin and that payment is enough;

it is sufficient, and it is finished. My part of this life-giving process is to simply accept the sacrifice that Jesus made on my behalf and the forgiveness that He offers.

One of the most damaging practices or requirements of conservative religious leaders is: don't hang out with sinners.

Sure, you can hand them a tract as long as you keep them at arms-length.

You can preach AT them as long as you don't get too close or stay too long.

You can pray for them, but don't be seen in public enjoying their company. They are, after all, contaminated and might spread that contamination on to you.

But what about the idea that we are loved unconditionally? That the price for our forgiveness has already been paid? That the Great King of Heaven loved us so deeply that He sacrificed His only Son to pay the ransom for us all? What list of requirements did Jesus have for becoming a child of God?

> *"Here I am! I stand at the door and knock. If anyone hears my voice and opens the door, I will come in and eat with that person, and they with me"* Revelation 3:20 NIV

> *"Ask and it will be given to you; seek and you will find; knock and the door will be opened to you"* Matthew 7:7 NIV

Jesus stands at the door and knocks and all we have to do is invite Him in. Simple. Maybe not easy, but simple. No long list of do's and don'ts, just respond to the knock on the door of your heart.

Let Him take it from there.

Jesus also said,

> *"Repent: for the kingdom of heaven is at hand"* Matthew 4:17 NIV

Repent. It seemed like a dreadful word to me.

What does it mean to repent? Even that simple word is often distorted by the list makers and rule keepers. Properly translated in this context, the word simply means, "Let God change the way you think."

Μετανοησατε (metanoeo), the original Greek word translated "repent," means to "change one's mind, attitude and purpose."

Let God change the way you think. Ask Him for new eyes to see and new ears to hear.

> For God so loved the world that He gave His one and only Son, that whoever believes in Him shall not perish but have eternal life.
> – John 3:16

He didn't wait for us to grovel, beg, and plead for our forgiveness to tolerate us grudgingly. Instead, we read in Romans:

> But God demonstrates His love for us in this: While we were still sinners, Christ died for us—Roman 5:8

Finally, we have the account in Acts 16 of Paul and Silas in jail. An angel came and opened their jail cell, but they did not try to run away. The jailer in charge would have been accountable if they had escaped, and he could have been put to death.

Paul and Silas in Prison:

> Once when we were going to the place of prayer, we were met by a female slave who had a spirit by which she predicted the future. She earned a great deal of money for her owners by fortune-telling. She followed Paul and the rest of us, shouting, "These men are servants of the Most-High God, who are telling you the way to be saved." She kept this up for many days. Finally, Paul became so annoyed that he turned around and said to the spirit, "In the name of Jesus Christ, I command you to come out of her!" At that moment, the spirit left her.
>
> When her owners realized that their hope of making money was gone, they seized Paul and Silas and dragged them into the marketplace to face the authorities. They brought them before the magistrates and said, "These men are Jews, and are throwing our city into an uproar by advocating customs unlawful for us Romans to accept or practice."

The crowd joined in the attack against Paul and Silas, and the magistrates ordered them to be stripped and beaten with rods. After they had been severely flogged, they were thrown into prison, and the jailer was commanded to guard them carefully. When he received these orders, he put them in the inner cell and fastened their feet in the stocks.

About midnight, Paul and Silas were praying and singing hymns to God, and the other prisoners were listening to them. Suddenly, there was such a violent earthquake that the foundations of the prison were shaken. At once, all the prison doors flew open and everyone's chains came loose. The jailer woke up, and when he saw the prison doors open, he drew his sword and was about to kill himself because he thought the prisoners had escaped. But Paul shouted, "Don't harm yourself! We are all here!"

The jailer called for lights, rushed in and fell trembling before Paul and Silas. He then brought them out and asked, "Sirs, what must I do to be saved?"

They replied, "Believe in the Lord Jesus and you will be saved—you and your household." Then they spoke the word of the Lord to him and to all the others in his house. At that hour of the night, the jailer took them and washed their wounds; then

immediately, he and all his household were baptized. The jailer brought them into his house and set a meal before them; he was filled with joy because he had come to believe in God—he and his whole household.
Acts 16: 16–40 NIV

What must I do to be saved? "Believe in the Lord Jesus Christ and you will be saved."

The list of do's and don'ts? The preconditions? The additional requirements established by the list makers? They are not there.

A WORD ABOUT PERSPECTIVE

Good Friday—2000 years ago, there was a man who was born in a dusty little village in the Middle East. This man spent his whole life taking care of and loving other people. He was the only man in the history of mankind to perfectly keep God's laws. He restored dignity to adulterers, extended friendship to the lowly, and sat down to dinner with prodigals. But, instead of receiving the Nobel Peace prize, he was falsely accused, wrongly arrested, improperly tried, unfairly convicted, and undeservedly sentenced to death. He was ruthlessly mocked, mercilessly beaten, cruelly tortured, brutally executed. . .and now we get the day off and celebrate by calling it Good Friday!

Does that sound like a day to be celebrated?

It all comes back to perspective. From one viewpoint, it was just another day in the life of a people and a city occupied by the Roman Empire. It was not the first execution in the city of Jerusalem and certainly not the last. The means of putting this man to death was intentionally cruel. Crucifixion was a method of execution meant to send a message to all who watched—*Don't mess with Rome*. Don't rock the boat and don't buck the religious elite (the Jewish elders).

However, from another perspective, this man of lowly birth and quiet integrity, uttered a single word in Aramaic that would usher in a new world order.

That one word? "Tetelestai."

That single word is translated into the English phrase, "It is finished."

With that word, the entire world changed. With that action, both the history and the ongoing story of man was concluded and reborn—all in one moment.

That moment came on that Friday afternoon when Jesus of Nazareth breathed his last.

"It is finished" marked the end of human history as it had been lived out for thousands of years.

A history of separation between God and man.

A history of man living in opposition to God.

A history of mankind living outside the relationship that God had intended from the beginning.

His life for my life.

His sacrifice redeemed me.

Paid my ransom.

Set me free.

He said, *"It is finished,"* and it was. All my sins, all my failures, all my brokenness, mistakes, shortcomings, and stubbornness were wiped away in that single act and sealed by that single word: *"Tetelestai."*

Everything that I have ever done that is less than it should be, was redeemed on that Friday afternoon. Nearly 2000 years ago, it was all paid for.

Tetelestai: it is finished.

Everything I have ever done and everything that I will ever do that contradicts God's law is forgiven.

I have been the prodigal son, certain that my Father in heaven was angry, certain that I deserved punishment and that the punishment was imminent. The truth of the matter is that I am forgiven and have been adopted into the family of God. I am both loved and delighted in by my Heavenly Father.

Now my challenge is to live my life as if I believe that it is true. As if I believe, understand, and accept that I am one of God's beloved children. Not merely tolerated or acknowledged, but beloved.

God loves me and adores me even more than I love and cherish my own children and grandchildren. As much as I love and care for them and would drop whatever I am doing for them, as much as I enjoy their presence when they visit, as much as I revel in their beauty and humor and accomplishments, more than all of that, God loves me. And He loves you too.

Can it be true? The God that I have come to know assures me that it is so. Yet, I struggle to believe it; I want to believe it and I believe it for you, but I often feel so unlovable and unworthy that I wonder how it could be so.

All I can tell you by way of explanation is that His Spirit assures me of His love, and I believe it. At least I believe it as I am writing this down and as I am sharing it with you.

And it is likely that tomorrow I will awaken and remember who I am, what I've done, and what I have failed to do. Then I will start all over. I will need to be reminded of His amazing grace again tomorrow. I will be assured by His Spirit that this outrageous love, this unreasonable affection directed at me and presented to me is true. The God who is the same yesterday, today and forever will testify that I am His.

Too good to be true?

Well, yes. . .

. . .and that is precisely what makes Good Friday so good.

Chapter 6

Shock and Awe

"The gospel declares that no matter how dutiful or prayerful we are, we can't save ourselves. What Jesus did was sufficient."

BRENNAN MANNING, *THE RAGAMUFFIN GOSPEL*[1]

LUTHER

MARTIN LUTHER CAME FROM a working-class family. His father, John Luther, an experienced German miner, was determined to see that his son was educated. At the age of 18, Martin Luther entered Erfurt University, seeking a law degree. The university proved to be a paradise of knowledge for the young man's inquisitive mind. He was drawn into studying the writings of great philosophers: Aristotle, Aquinas, Cicero, Virgo, and many others.

His studies were feeding the skills of logical understanding, agility of thought, and talent for language. He spent many hours in the university library drinking in the wisdom offered in its many

1. Manning, *Ragamuffin Gospel.*

volumes. It was here that Luther made a lifechanging discovery. As he combed through the books, one by one, he came across a book he had never seen before—The Bible.

James A. Wylie records the discovery:

> *"The Bible he had never seen till now. His joy was great. There are certain portions which the Church prescribes to be read in public on Sundays and saints' days, and Luther imagined that these were the whole Bible. His surprise was great when, on opening the volume, he found in it whole books and epistles of which he had never before heard. He began to read with the feelings of one to whom the heavens have been opened."*[2]

He was elated to learn that instead of just a few standardized prayers, short Bible passages, and church rituals and practices, there were sixty-six books written by "holy men of God (who) spoke *as they were moved by the Holy Spirit*." 2 Peter 1:21 NKJV

After years of diligent work on Luther's part, he graduated as a Doctor of Philosophy from Erfurt University. It was a great accomplishment and held the promise of a prosperous future. But he was in for an electrifying experience!

During a break in his studies, Luther traveled home to Mansfield to see his parents. After a time, he returned to Erfurt. As he approached the city gate the sky rapidly grew dark, the clouds were black and it began to thunder and lightning. It was unlike any storm he had ever experienced. Suddenly, a bolt of lightning struck the ground close by with a power and a force so terrible that it knocked him to the ground. At that moment, he felt as if the Great Judge of Heaven had arrived with the clouds, and he was certain that he would be struck dead. In his terror, he made a solemn vow to God—that if God would spare him, he would spend the remainder of his life in his service. With that vow, the storm rumbled past. Luther picked himself up from the ground and entered the city gates of Erfurt.

---

2. Wylie, *History of Protestantism*, 233.2.

A promise is a promise, a vow is a vow. Even with a future as an affluent lawyer or prominent judge ahead of him, Luther kept his vow and entered the monastery.

One would suppose that within the quiet halls of the monastery, Luther would find peace. That is what Luther himself expected. That was not to be. In the convent, his conscience barked and howled more loudly than ever before. He was still trying to find life in his own good works not in the finished work of Christ. The panic began to build within his spirit more with each passing day. What could he do? Where could he go to find rest for his soul? If comfort was not to be found in penance, confession, self-denial, and service, then he was indeed hopelessly lost.

Luther struggled for months and then years, trying, by his works, to appease what he believed to be an angry God. He tried every established practice, praying for hours on end, reading the Bible day and night, and fasting until nearly dying of malnutrition. Still, he could not find the acceptance he so desperately sought.

Luther was convinced and determined to get it right, but to do it on his terms. It was with both pride and stubbornness that that he returned again and again to the door of heaven.

> Alas, the poor monk! What shall he do? He can think but of longer fasts, of severer penances, of more numerous prayers. He returns a third time. Surely, he will now be admitted? Alas, no! the sum is yet too small; the door is still shut; justice demands a still larger price. He returns again and again, and always with a bigger sum in his hand; but the door is not opened. God is teaching him that heaven is not to be bought by any sum, however great: that eternal life is the free gift of God. -Wylie[3]

Where would it all end? What else could he do to earn the salvation and grace for which he so fervently searched?

How could he ever satisfy the requirements of a holy God?

Where would he find forgiveness?

In the same place I did.

In surrender.

3. Wylie, *History of Protestantism*, 234.1.

It was not in penitence. It was not in the confessional. It was not in sacrifice.

It was in surrender.

For many years, I was aware of my shortcomings and wayward inclinations, and just in case I should forget, the church regularly reminded me of my sin. And with every reminder of my faults came a renewed commitment to get it right. To do more to make up for my failures. To strive harder to please God with my good works.

And in the struggle, I found no relief. None.

When I failed, I tried harder. Nothing.

Self-discipline was not the answer.

Generosity? Zero.

Contrition, guilt, groveling before God? Zilch.

And finally, I came to the end of myself. I'd had enough.

I confess, I'm not proud of my response to this failure. I had faced many challenges in my life, and I had managed to fight my way through them. I'd never been a quitter.

But now, in the most important quest in my life, I had failed. And do you want to know my response to that failure?

I quit.

I didn't surrender. I didn't say, "God, please help me." I just simply said, "I quit." I can tell you exactly where I was sitting when I gave up. To this day, I can still feel the weight of that moment. I despised the word *surrender*. It smacked of failure and weakness.

I quit.

I sat down in the middle of the religious highway, and I stopped. There was nothing noble about it. I didn't surrender to a higher power. I didn't go forward in response to an emotional altar call. I didn't raise my hands and say, "Lord help me."

I just quit. And even though I hated the word surrender, I recognize it now for what it was. I indeed acknowledged that I'd had enough. I surrendered.

At that moment, I sensed the voice of God say, "Well, it's about time. I've been waiting for you to come to the end of yourself. This has never been about what you do, good or bad. It's always been about what I have done for you. I love you and have a place for you and a purpose for your life. Come home."

By grace alone.

I didn't deserve it.

I didn't earn it.

It was a gift from a loving Father to a wayward son.

Martin Luther, too, traversed a long and painful journey in his quest to "get it right."

John Staupitz was a clergyman in Germany, and he was unique in that he was among the few who understood God's simple plan of salvation. Being led by the Spirit of God, Staupitz chose to place his trust not in the church, but Christ alone. Spiritually speaking, Europe in the fourteenth century was a dark place. In the midst of this darkness, Staupitz and a small band of brothers saw the light of the gospel and followed it.

It happened then that Vicar Staupitz undertook a tour of the convents and monasteries in Germany. Upon his arrival at the monastery in Erfurt, he met Martin Luther. With discernment powered by the Holy Spirit, Staupitz was intrigued. He saw a deep sadness on Luther's face, an anguish of soul that indicated an intense inner struggle. By this time, Luther was emaciated and weak as a result of his fasting and praying in his quest for righteousness. Staupitz himself had experienced the bitter cup of self that Luther was now drinking from. The Vicar shared the good news of the gospel with Luther, but Luther replied, "I cannot and dare not come to God until I am a better man. I have not yet repented sufficiently."

Staupitz replied, "A better man? Christ came to save not good men but sinners. They that are whole need not a physician, but those that are sick. Love God and you will have repented. There is no real repentance that does not begin in the love of God. We love Him because He first loved us. God offers mercy and freedom from sin through the blood of Christ. Have faith in the mercy of God! We are not saved by righteous works that we have done but by His mercy and grace. He saved us and renewed us through the Holy Ghost."

Before the vicar departed from Luther, he gave him the gift of a Bible and said, "Let the study of the scriptures be your favorite occupation. Man shall not live by bread alone, but by every word that proceeds from the mouth of God."[4]

Martin Luther had a difficult time getting his eyes off himself and his shortcomings and he fell into a deep state of depression. He became so sick that he was near death. It was in this state that a brother monk in the monastery prayed with him and shared with him the Apostles' Creed. He encouraged Luther to say it out loud with him:

> *I believe in God, the Father Almighty, Creator of Heaven and earth; and in Jesus Christ, His only Son Our Lord,*
>
> *Who was conceived by the Holy Spirit, born of the Virgin Mary, suffered under Pontius Pilate, was crucified, died, and was buried. He descended into Hell; the third day He rose again from the dead; He ascended into Heaven, and sitteth at the right hand of God, the Father almighty; from thence He shall come to judge the living and the dead.*
>
> *I believe in the Holy Spirit, the holy catholic church, the communion of saints, the forgiveness of sins, the resurrection of the body and life everlasting. Amen.*

When Luther repeated *"I believe in the forgiveness of sins. . ."* the monk reminded him it was not just David's sins or Peter's sins, but Luther's own sins had been forgiven too. It was almost like scales fell from his eyes. Finally, Luther could see the light! That one phrase in the Apostles' Creed finally took hold in his heart, and in that tiny room of the monastery, Luther the monk died, and Luther the Christian was born!

So how did things work out for Martin Luther?

He became the Father of the Reformation.

He fought to make the Word of God available to all people in their own language. By publishing a translation of the Bible, he made the teachings and example of Jesus accessible to many.

---

4. Wylie, *History of Protestantism.*

He recaptured the sacredness of all vocations as he confirmed that any work conducted in faith was an opportunity to reflect the Creator and love his neighbor.

He wrote many of the hymns we sing today in Protestant churches and created several catechisms so that we may better understand the Word of God.

Luther is regarded as one of the most influential figures in the history of Christianity.

So, what does this all mean for you? Just this—you are more than just a redeemed wayward son or daughter. You are a child of the King. You have gifts and talents that the world needs, and you have a divinely appointed destiny! What will God do in your life when you come to the place of surrender?

Chapter 7

Salvation is for Dead People

"He has a single relentless stance toward us: He loves us. He is the only God man has ever heard of who loves sinners."

BRENNAN MANNING[1]

SOMEHOW IN THE PROCESS of communicating God's great love toward us, the idea of life after death has become a nearly exclusive focal point for some in the institutional Church. The premise or truth that God has prepared a place for us that's better than here, other than here, is certainly true.

Jesus said,

> *"In my father's house are many mansions: if it were not so, I would have told you. I go to prepare a place for you"*
> -John 14:2 KJV

In addition, there are numerous references to Heaven describing it as the home of God—a place with mansions and streets of gold, the residence of angels and the seat or throne of God. While all of these statements contain the truth, considered in

1. Manning, *Ragamuffin Gospel.*

isolation they only convey part of the truth. If the focus of our lives is limited to getting to Heaven after we die, then the scope and content of our lives will be limited as well. If we believe that the quality of our heavenly experience depends solely on how we live our earthly lives, then we will either spend our lives in a frantic push to "earn our rewards in heaven" and get "more jewels in our crown" or, recognizing that we don't measure up, resign ourselves to a second class citizenship when we get to Heaven and live a life of quiet despair here on earth.

Often, in the conservative, fundamentalist religious community, there is the idea that the world is getting worse and worse, and that our planet will eventually end in cataclysm or apocalypse. Since it is all going to be destroyed anyway, the main function in life is to "hang on" until Jesus comes or until we die.

Another danger of reserving salvation just for dead people is the bunker mentality. This is the idea that the world is full of wickedness and that our only hope is to hide out in our religious bunker, surrounded by similarly minded bunker dwellers, and hold on long enough to be "raptured" or until we die. Bunker dwellers suffer this earthly existence in stoic, pious holiness, "hunkering down" to avoid being tempted or soiled by the world around them. The underlying hope of this mentality is that they'll get to start over in a better place after they are dead.

While both responses to the lie contain elements of the truth, they leave out the essence of the good news of the gospel:

That our salvation begins *now*.

That our new life begins *now*.

That we are in the process of pioneering His kingdom *now*.

The truth is that the Kingdom of God is not just "up there" and it's not reserved only for dead people. The truth is that Jesus brought the Kingdom of Heaven here to earth. The truth is that as we recognize His great love for us, we will respond to the world around us in love. As we do that, we begin to establish God's kingdom here and now. Reconciliation with God occurred at the cross and when Jesus rose from the dead, a new age dawned. Jesus himself said, *"The Kingdom of Heaven is at hand."*

The Kingdom of Heaven is now, and we have a place in it and a part to play in building it. It is not just something to dream about after we die. It is something that we can take part in today. Our existence does not cease after we die. We recognize that. But it is also not just a reboot or start over, it is a continuation of who we are and who we have spent our earthly lives becoming. It is a realization of all that we were designed to be, prior to our conception, through our earthly birth and over the course of our human existence, extending into our heavenly eternity.

The notion of "just hang on" robs us of joy, of living in the here and now with purpose. It forces us to focus only on the future at the expense of living today for today.

According to the Westminster confession of faith, the chief duty of man is to "Glorify God and enjoy Him forever." Forever doesn't just begin after we die; forever starts now.

Remember the tapestry: from the back, we see hundreds or thousands of tiny threads. These threads are all of different colors, whether bright or dark, colorful or muted- each thread is pointing in a different direction. It looks like a scrambled disorganized mess. But flip the tapestry over and you can see that what once appeared to be random threads, when looked at from the right perspective, from the intended angle, form a beautiful work of art. Looked at from the proper vantage point, we can see that every one of those seemingly random threads is essential to the finished work of art that is the subject of the tapestry. The same can be said of you and I, each generation that came before us, our children, and our children's children. Each of us discovering and deploying our individual passions and talents is critical to the story of humanity.

I had an acquaintance who had experienced a great deal of rejection, trauma, and loss in her life, including an attempt on her life and the murder of her husband. I will refer to my friend as Martha for the purpose of this illustration.

Because of her life experiences, Martha was determined to control all aspects of her existence. At age 50, she went back to school and got a nursing degree. She controlled the money and resources she had very carefully. In addition to working in health care, she began to lend out the money she had saved at a rate of 18% to people who were desperate enough to pay the interest rate. When she inherited some money, she loaned that out as well and was on her way to considerable wealth. But it wasn't just money she controlled. She tried to control each conversation and interaction she had. Additionally, she didn't like children. She didn't have any of her own and didn't tolerate being around the kids of other people. In short, her response to the trauma in her life was to seek shelter in controlling her environment and everyone in it.

Martha had no use for religion. If the topic came up in conversation, she immediately tried to change the conversation and if that didn't work, she just closed up. At the age of 79, she was diagnosed with terminal melanoma. Over the years that we knew each other, we had developed an unspoken truce. I would do my best not to introduce religion into every conversation and she did her best to avoid blowing up when the subject did arise.

With her terminal diagnosis, I knew the truce would have to end. I knew that she did not believe in God or an afterlife, but I felt compelled to share with her the story of our fallen nature, and of our rescue and redemption. I stopped by to see her shortly after she received the bad news from her doctor. I asked her if we could talk for a few minutes about something important. We went down to a quiet conference room in the library of her assisted living facility and I told her that I wanted to talk with her about what comes "next."

Her response was, "There is nothing next. We die and it's all over. That's the end."

We had known each other for more than 30 years and I knew that she didn't want to talk about religion. On the other hand, she knew that I believed in God and in His son, Jesus, and that heaven is somewhere down the road for each of us.

"But Martha, what if, for once, I'm right and you're wrong?"

She relented and allowed me to share the story of God and the gospel with her. I did my very best to present the information logically and passionately. When I thought I had covered all the bases to the best of my ability, I asked her what she thought. Her response?

"Well, that's fine for you, but I don't believe any of it."

Period.

End of discussion.

A few days later, a nurse who worked in the health care section of the home approached me. She had overheard me sharing the story of the gospel with Martha and asked if it would be ok if she followed up with her.

I asked the nurse if she had seen Martha's written directives, that she wanted no religion mentioned at her passing. A pastor was not to be called. She specified that it be recorded she was an atheist. No religion. Period.

The nurse responded, "I've seen her chart and the instructions, but I feel I need to reach out one last time."

I replied with; "Ok, you know the risks, go ahead and give it a try."

Martha died a week later.

I attended a "memory service" in Martha's honor. Some of the people she knew met together in a room to share fond memories and the funny stories of their time with her. Just before I stepped into the room, the nurse who had wanted to talk with Martha beckoned me over.

"Yesterday, I asked Martha if she was ready to receive Jesus, and she said, 'Yes!'"

She said yes.

Yes, to a God who had pursued her for 79 years and 361 days.

Pursued her with love, with grace, with mercy.

Relentlessly.

And she said "Yes."

I was dumb struck. Martha had finally found the love of Jesus in her very last days. Like the thief on the cross to whom Jesus said, *"this day you will be with me in paradise."* I would be seeing Martha again and that was good news.

But as I reflected on her transformation, I was saddened by another reality. Martha had lived for more than 79 years seeking only her own needs, wants, and desires. She had controlled her existence but was miserable for much of her life.

What a loss!

In that moment, I realized another truth. Salvation isn't only about the next life: it impacts the way we live this life too.

At a personal level, God had revealed Himself to me at a time when I had the great majority of my life still ahead of me. Because I came to know Him early on, I am now able to live a life of love and purpose and joy. I get the best of this life and the next one too! I regard it as a profound privilege to have found meaning and happiness in this life, even while I look forward to the next.

Make no mistake. I look forward to celebrating the joy and adventures of heaven. But, by the grace and mercy of God, I can be fully present for the triumphs and trials of this life as well.

Salvation is not just for dead people after all!

> "Truly, I say to you, unless you turn and become like children, you will never enter the kingdom of heaven"
> -Matthew 18:3 ESV

Chapter 8

A Brave New World

"But if I've learned anything about the world of grace, it's that failure is always a chance for a do-over."

BRENNAN MANNING[1]

"This is how the birth of Jesus Christ came about: His mother Mary was pledged to be married to Joseph, but before they came together, she was found to be with child through the Holy Spirit."

– MATTHEW 1:18 NIV

THE RESCUE PLAN OF God was entering a new season. After allowing us to "do our own thing" for thousands of years. God was prepared to go to extremes to redeem those He loved—You and me. Our first parents failed to keep their covenant with God—they broke the contract.

In the person of Jesus, God came to live with us and do for us what we could not do for ourselves.

---

1. Manning and Blasé, *All Is Grace.*

As a being that was fully God and fully man, Jesus kept the original contract. To do so, Jesus looked to God the Father to guide His words and deeds. He was subject to every temptation we experience, but He chose to live His human life in cooperation with the Holy Spirit and His Father in heaven. He was thereby empowered to live a sinless life.

D-DAY IN DECEMBER

Having been a high school history teacher for better than two decades, I hope my students can recall the significance of D-Day: June 6, 1944. It was the day Allied forces in World War Two landed on the beaches of Normandy. Although a dark portent of things to come, its beginning signaled the end of a brutal war that cost millions of lives.

Each time the Christmas season comes around, I am reminded of another D-Day of sorts. Another day when a courageous leader stepped ashore, into the midst of a battle that would ultimately cost him his life. A quiet, humble, and kind hero that would lead an unlikely, rag-tag bunch of followers into a type of warfare that the world had never seen before. His followers were armed only with love but were willing to fight to the death.

That fateful day signified not only the inception of a difficult but eventually victorious campaign, it signaled the dawn of a whole new world, a world where goodness will reign and where that good brings peace and equity to all people.

A world that knows no divide between rich and poor, no tension between ethnic groups, no exploitation of the weak and powerless.

A world where "mine" has been replaced with "ours."

A world where "me" has been exchanged for "we."

A world where evil is overpowered by goodness and truth.

A world conscious of justice, a world capable of mercy, and a world awash in grace.

Yes, we celebrate that day and the life of the one who stepped into the world to subdue and destroy evil.

We celebrate the ongoing work to restore love, grace, and justice in our world.

Although the battle is not yet complete, we live with the promise that His victory is sure. My friends and I will join billions of other followers of Christ as we celebrate His quiet, meek, and understated arrival on December 25th as the pre-cursor to the greatest victory the world has ever known.

"The Kingdom of heaven is at hand. . ." -Matthew 4:17 NIV

To this teacher, the birth of Jesus is a lot like D-Day in WWII, and that is pretty cool. Once the Allied forces landed on the beaches of France, the outcome of the war was on the horizon. It would take ten months of hard, bloody, vicious fighting to reach Berlin, but the end of Nazi domination and cruelty was near.

In the same way, once the great God of the universe arrived in Bethlehem of Judea, the end of evil was in sight. Satan knew that his reign was in jeopardy, and he inspired Herod to commit genocide, but Jesus escaped and a new world order was in the making.

"In the beginning was the Word, and the Word was with God, and the Word was God." -John 1:1 NIV

For many, John's reference to this verse back in Genesis reflects the beginning of all things. But could it also be referring to a fresh new beginning? The beginning of a new creation and a new world order— a renewal of all things with creation restored? Something new, something big, something different that God is doing through Jesus and ultimately Jesus will do through you and me?

The death of Jesus wasn't the end of hope. On the contrary, it signified the fulfillment of God's promise to make all things right again. It signaled the beginning, the defeat of Satan, and the start of everything. It was the new thing.

What will it take to establish a new world? Simply put—share the good news of the Gospel, tell the truth.

What springs to life because of the truth?

A city on a hill, where everyone has enough. Where commerce is encouraged, and environmental stewardship is the vision. Where no one is oppressed.

What will it take to make a world where everyone has enough?

Sacrifice, sharing what we have, doing the things that God has called us to do.

When Jesus came to speak the truth, He came to tell the world of "the new world order"—the paradigm of accomplished redemption. The truth He came to speak of was that the time had come for God to set the world right with Himself. Because of the work of Jesus, God has blotted out our sins.

> *For as high as the heavens are above the earth, so great is*
> *his love for those who fear him; as far as the east is from*
> *the west, so far has he removed our transgressions from us.*
> -Psalm 103:11–12 NIV

It is a certainty that the God who created the universe could accomplish all of this and more without our help. But He chooses to do His work through us, though flawed and unremarkable as we are.

But it is this shade of difference, this degree of separation that makes the message so powerful and alive. He is not waiting on us. He is already on the move! We are reconciled already. If we but knew it and believed it so that we could live as if it were true!

Those who said, "Take Him away, crucify Him" were in fact, saying, "No, no! We don't want a new world order. We don't want to be reconciled on God's terms. We want to remain in control! We want to determine and dispense the truth. We want to call the shots, even if it costs us everything!"

But the resurrection of Jesus changed everything. He has become the sacrifice to atone for our sins, and in His death on the cross, He paid our ransom. He suffered and died so that we could live. In His resurrection, He signaled that His sacrifice was sufficient for the forgiveness of our sins.

When Jesus rose from the dead, He proved that He was the Son of God. Furthermore, He established that God is sovereign over life and death, and His resurrection guarantees eternal life for all believers.

It also has important implications for us regarding our earthly life. By His death and resurrection, we know that the death of our bodies is not the end for us. Armed with this knowledge, we can invest our lives in the work of God, knowing that it will have eternal implications for us and for those we serve.

Apostle Paul says this in I Corinthians 15.

> *"Therefore, my dear brothers and sisters, stand firm. Let nothing move you. Always give yourselves fully to the work of the Lord, because you know that your labor in the Lord is not in vain"* NIV

The resurrection is the triumphant and glorious victory for every believer. Jesus Christ died, was buried, and rose the third day according to the Scriptures. And He is coming again! The dead in Christ will be raised up, and along with those who are alive at His coming will receive new, glorified bodies.

Why is the resurrection of Jesus Christ important? It proves who Jesus is. It demonstrates that God accepted Jesus' sacrifice on our behalf. It shows that God has the power to raise us from the dead. It guarantees that the bodies of those who believe in Christ will not remain dead but will be resurrected unto eternal life.

The journey has already begun. The Kingdom is already here. Don't expend your life only waiting for life in the hereafter. Our redemption has already been accomplished, our joy begins now! The victory has been won and death is already defeated. The resurrection of Jesus was the starting whistle and the signal that eternity starts now!

Don't wait to enjoy a new life, because that new life begins today.

Where do we start?

> *"Do to others as you would have them do to you"* Luke 6:31 NIV

LOVE FOR NEIGHBOR DURING DARK DAYS

It's heartwarming to see one of the dark times in our nation's history bring about an example of the golden rule.

It all began with an executive order signed in 1942 by President Franklin D. Roosevelt that removed some 120,000 people of Japanese descent living in the United States from their homes and placed them in internment camps. The justification was that there was danger of those of Japanese descent spying for our enemy at the time: the empire of Japan. However, more than two-thirds of those interned were American citizens and half of them were children. None had ever shown disloyalty to the United States of America.

In some cases, family members were separated and put in different camps-most of these camps there located in the West, including some here in Arizona.

January 2, 1945, officially marked the end of the Japanese internment during World War II.

On Father's Day, I read an older copy of Reader's Digest that referenced that dark time in our country's history. Here's where the golden rule moment surrounding that story comes in.

It happened in California when a Japanese family was taken to the internment camps near Casa Grande. The neighbor of the Japanese family owned a vineyard and grew grapes for the many wineries close by, as did the family who had been interned.

Both had been close friends since moving to that area and both were successful growers. It was quite a blow to the Japanese family to leave their vineyards, fearing that all that had gone into their profitable enterprise would be lost. But that was not to be. Soon after the Japanese family had been removed from their farm, his friend next door took it upon himself to preserve his neighbor's vineyard so that, upon his return, it would be just as he left it.

Consequently, during those three years that his neighbor was interned, this man and his sons pruned, harvested, and did whatever needed to be done on his neighbor's farm to preserve and care for that vineyard along with his own. It was double work for three years, but because of his love for his neighbor, he persevered.

The story, as told by his son, recounts the many times during those years that he told his dad just to give it up because it was so much work. Yet, his dad always told him that he would want his neighbor to do the same for him.

During that interim, he not only cared for the vineyard, but he kept up the lawns, the gardens, and even painted the house and outbuildings. He wanted to be sure that they were in perfect condition, just as his neighbor had left them.

What his son didn't know and was not revealed until the neighbor returned was that, during those three years that he and his dad and siblings were caring for that neighbor's vineyard, his father was careful to keep accurate records of everything that was harvested and sold during his absence. He also deposited all the money into a savings account for his neighbor, so when the family returned to their vineyard, it was as though they had never left.

One can only imagine the wonderful surprise awaiting them when that Japanese family returned to their home! The house was in excellent condition. The vineyard was just as bountiful and fruitful. There was money in the bank earning interest. The garden products had been canned and preserved. The lawn was cut, the house was painted, and everything was found in perfect order—as it was when they left.

> It almost sounds like a story out of a fairytale. But it is indeed a true story shared by a son who recalled how his father modeled the Golden Rule during a very difficult time in our nation's history. -Rev. Larry Fultz.[2]

THE LIFE OF JESUS

If Adam and Eve broke the contract, then Jesus fulfilled it. Jesus came to do for us what we could not do for ourselves. He lived a perfect life in dependence on and in cooperation with His Father in Heaven.

2. Taylor, "Man Showed Love for His Neighbor."

We often overlook the life of Jesus and see only His sacrificial death and subsequent resurrection. The initial part of His mission was to live life as we were supposed to live in the first place.

According to Apostle Paul in the second chapter of Philippians, Jesus humbled Himself to come to our rescue:

> ". . .have the same mindset as Christ Jesus: Who, being in very nature God, did not consider equality with God something to be used to his own advantage; rather, he made himself nothing by taking the very nature of a servant, being made in human likeness. And being found in appearance as a man, he humbled himself by becoming obedient to death— even death on a cross!" Philippians 2: 5–8 NIV

Jesus not only technically fulfilled the terms of the contract, He showed us what was possible, what could have been, and best of all, what could still be yet!

Jesus entered our world as a baby only after emptying Himself "of all but love." He subjected Himself to His parents, learned and grew in wisdom and stature and in favor with God and man. The one who was fully God intentionally emptied Himself and became fully man so that we might fully live.

Christ's life here on earth was only 33 years long. But in those years, He changed the course of history for all of humankind.

ACTIONS SPEAK LOUDER THAN WORDS

Jesus' public ministry was only three years in length, and in those years, He proclaimed, by word and action, that God had come to live among us. To give us an example of living a life of righteousness, love, and service. Not only did He give us a model to follow, He also demonstrated that He was God in the flesh, and proved His claims through life, death, and resurrection.

Three years is not a long time to leave your mark on the world. Yet, no other figure in history has had as great an impact on our world and our culture than Jesus of Nazareth. His influence was so notable that the calendar in use for over two thousand years separates history into two periods: BC (Before Christ) and AD (Anno Domini, In the year of our Lord).

The Christian Bible has sold more copies than any other book in history, estimated to be over 5 billion copies.

No other leader has had more influence on our culture's history and our present than Jesus.

Early in His ministry, when asked if He was "the one" or the long-awaited Messiah, He chose to point to what He was doing rather than make the direct statement that He was the divine Son of God.

He would make that claim when the time was right.

So, what did He do during His short period of ministry? He proved that He was all that He claimed to be; that He was all-sufficient to affect our rescue, redemption, and reconciliation with God and with His creation.

He studied and explained the scriptures so that people could understand that a new way of life was possible and that a new kingdom had come. He controlled the wind and the waves, healed the sick, purged the temple of thieves and religious charlatans, turned water into wine, walked on water, and fed the hungry by faith. He freed people from the control of demons, healed people of their diseases, and raised people from the dead.

He did things that only God could do.

And what did He say to you and me?

He invited us to receive forgiveness, experience our own healing, and join Him in the work of this new kingdom.

In Matthew chapter 6, He says:

> "But seek first His kingdom and His righteousness, and all these things will be given to you as well. Therefore, do not worry about tomorrow, for tomorrow will worry about itself. Each day has enough trouble of its own." NIV

And in Mark 16:15

> He said to them, "Go into all the world and preach the gospel to all creation." NIV

Also, Revelation 3:20:

*"Behold, I stand at the door and knock. If anyone hears
my voice and opens the door, I will come in to him and eat
with him, and he with me"* ESV

He invites us to open the door of our hearts and to ask Him
to come in. When we do open that door, He gives us a new heart
of flesh to replace our heart of stone. He gives us new eyes with
which to see the world and new ears to hear what is going on
around us. When we open that door and "repent," we are asking
Him to change the way we think, and He offers us the priceless gift
of salvation.

But what Jesus brings does not end with our forgiveness. He
also charges us with the adventure of sharing the good news of
our redemption and reconciliation to God with the whole world.
Further, He did not just set an example for us of what love and
service and sacrifice look like. When He ascended into heaven
after His crucifixion and resurrection, He promised to send us
someone who would give us the power to live this new life in His
new kingdom.

He sent to us the Holy Spirit to be our guide and our com-
forter. He sent the Holy Spirit to give us the power and the means
to follow the example of Jesus and to begin the building of His
kingdom.

This is revolutionary!

Let me state it again. He sent the Holy Spirit to give us the
power and the means to follow the example of Jesus and to begin
the building of His kingdom!

This, my friend, changes everything. We are not left to our
own devices to figure it all out, and we are no longer solely depen-
dent on our own strength and stamina to carry out all that God
has in store for us.

In the Gospel of John, chapter 14, Jesus made a promise to
all who believe:

*"And I will ask the Father, and he will give you another
advocate to help you and be with you forever— the Spirit
of truth. The world cannot accept Him, because it neither*

sees Him nor knows Him. But you know Him, for He lives with you and will be in you." NIV

The Holy Spirit has come and will be our power source to accomplish all that God has called us to do. To give us new strength, day by day, to assist in building the Kingdom of Heaven.

So, what is this new kingdom? Jesus explains it in the Sermon on the Mount which is recorded in Matthew:

> *"Now when Jesus saw the crowds, He went up on a mountainside and sat down. His disciples came to Him, and He began to teach them.*
> *He said:*
> *"Blessed are the poor in spirit,*
> *for theirs is the kingdom of heaven.*
> *Blessed are those who mourn,*
> *for they will be comforted.*
> *Blessed are the meek,*
> *for they will inherit the earth. Blessed are those who hunger and thirst for righteousness, for they will be filled.*
> *Blessed are the merciful,*
> *for they will be shown mercy.*
> *Blessed are the pure in heart,*
> *for they will see God.*
> *Blessed are the peacemakers,*
> *for they will be called children of God.*
> *Blessed are those who are persecuted because of righteousness,*
> *for theirs is the kingdom of heaven.*
> *"Blessed are you when people insult you, persecute you and falsely say all kinds of evil against you because of me. Rejoice and be glad, because great is your reward in heaven, for, in the same way, they persecuted the prophets who were before you.*
> *"You are the salt of the earth. But if the salt loses its saltiness, how can it be made salty again? It is no longer good for anything except to be thrown out and trampled underfoot.*
> *"You are the light of the world. A town built on a hill cannot be hidden. Neither do people light a lamp and put it under a bowl. Instead, they put it on its stand, and it*

gives light to everyone in the house. In the same way, let your light shine before others, that they may see your good deeds and glorify your Father in heaven." Matthew 5 NIV

Jesus fulfilled all requirements of the law to be our Redeemer:

"Do not think that I have come to abolish the Law or the Prophets; I have not come to abolish them but to fulfill them. For truly I tell you, until heaven and earth disappear, not the smallest letter, not the least stroke of a pen, will by any means disappear from the Law until everything is accomplished. Therefore, anyone who sets aside one of the least of these commands and teaches others accordingly will be called least in the Kingdom of Heaven, but whoever practices and teaches these commands will be called great in the Kingdom of Heaven. For I tell you that unless your righteousness surpasses that of the Pharisees and the teachers of the law, you will certainly not enter the Kingdom of Heaven."

MURDER

"You have heard that it was said to the people long ago, 'You shall not murder, and anyone who murders will be subject to judgment.' But I tell you that anyone who is angry with a brother or sister will be subject to judgment. Again, anyone who says to a brother or sister, 'You are worthless is answerable to the court. And anyone who says, 'You fool!' will be in danger of the fire of hell."

"Therefore, if you are offering your gift at the altar and there remember that your brother or sister has something against you, leave your gift there in front of the altar. First, go and be reconciled to them; then come and offer your gift."

"Settle matters quickly with your adversary who is taking you to court. Do it while you are still together on the way, or your adversary may hand you over to the judge, and the judge may hand you over to the officer, and you

may be thrown into prison. Truly I tell you, you will not get out until you have paid the last penny."

ADULTERY

"You have heard that it was said, 'You shall not commit adultery.' But I tell you that anyone who looks at a woman lustfully has already committed adultery with her in his heart. If your right eye causes you to stumble, gouge it out and throw it away. It is better for you to lose one part of your body than for your whole body to be thrown into hell. And if your right hand causes you to stumble, cut it off and throw it away. It is better for you to lose one part of your body than for your whole body to go into hell."

DIVORCE

"It has been said, 'Anyone who divorces his wife must give her a certificate of divorce.' But I tell you that anyone who divorces his wife, except for sexual immorality, makes her the victim of adultery.

OATHS

"Again, you have heard that it was said to the people long ago, 'Do not break your oath, but fulfill to the Lord the vows you have made.' But I tell you, do not swear an oath at all: either by heaven, for it is God's throne; or by the earth, for it is his footstool; or by Jerusalem, for it is the city of the Great King. And do not swear by your head, for you cannot make even one hair white or black. All you need to say is simply 'Yes' or 'No'; anything beyond this comes from the evil one."

EYE FOR EYE

> "You have heard that it was said, 'Eye for eye, and tooth for tooth.' But I tell you, do not resist an evil person. If anyone slaps you on the right cheek, turn to them the other cheek also. And if anyone wants to sue you and take your shirt, hand over your coat as well. If anyone forces you to go one mile, go with them two miles. Give to the one who asks you, and do not turn away from the one who wants to borrow from you."

LOVE FOR ENEMIES

> "You have heard that it was said, 'Love your neighbor and hate your enemy.' But I tell you, love your enemies and pray for those who persecute you, that you may be children of your Father in heaven. He causes his sun to rise on the evil and the good, and sends rain on the righteous and the unrighteous. If you love those who love you, what reward will you get? Are not even the tax collectors doing that? And if you greet only your own people, what are you doing more than others? Do not even pagans do that? Be perfect, therefore, as your heavenly Father is perfect."

Jesus gives us a detailed explanation of what it looks like to be His disciple and to serve as a member of this Kingdom of Heaven.

Jesus emphasized subjects such as prayer, justice, and caring for the poor and sick among us. He taught that it is what is in our hearts that matters. He said the real issue isn't murder, but anger. That it's not about swearing an oath, it's about speaking the truth even when it is inconvenient. He said it isn't about divorce but about keeping your word. The real problem isn't adultery, but instead it is desiring someone who isn't your spouse. He taught that we should turn the other cheek rather than demanding an eye for an eye. In addition to loving those we care about, we should also love our enemies. Finally, the real treasure we should concern ourselves with is not silver and gold but our new home in heaven.

In the end, Jesus made it clear that His followers should live in a much different way than others who don't know about Him and His kingdom. He preached that we should,

"*Let our lives so shine among men that they may see your good works and glorify God in heaven.*" Matthew 5:16 KJV

He didn't abolish God's commandments. Rather, He explained how to honor them faithfully.

First, Love God with all your heart, soul, and mind.

Second, Love your neighbor as yourself.

In His life, death and resurrection, Jesus does more than grant us the gift of forgiveness and the standing of redeemed sinners. Rather than just cleaning up our filthy rags, He gave us new clothes as white as snow. We are not just pardoned criminals. We are the beloved children of God, sons and daughters of our Heavenly Father with whom He is well pleased.

Paul reminds us in the first chapter of Ephesians that with our new status as children of the king, we have been unconditionally loved, forgiven, redeemed, chosen by God, and adopted into His family. We are blameless and reconciled, and we have the promise of spending eternity with God.

When we enter into the mindset of the Kingdom of God, our status is no longer confined to our accomplishments in the workplace or our political party. In God's kingdom, our character is not determined by gender or ethnicity, or even the approval of our family and friends. When we anchor our hearts in the promises of God, we find new freedom to engage each sphere of life with courage and purpose. Our identity is certain, we have been adopted into the family of God and our names are written in the Lamb's Book of Life.

In short, Jesus sets us free to live and enjoy a new, meaningful and bountiful life, in His kingdom, the Kingdom of Heaven.

What was Jesus' mission statement?

"*The Spirit of the Lord is upon me, because He has anointed me to bring good news to the poor. He has sent me to proclaim release to the captives and recovery of sight to the*

blind, to let the oppressed go free, to proclaim the year of
the Lord's favor" Luke 4:18–19 ESV

While I am not fully man and fully God like Jesus, I can, by the power of the Holy Spirit, bring good news to the poor, proclaim release to the captives, and help the blind recover their sight. I can work to set the oppressed free from their oppressors, and I can proclaim to everyone the love, forgiveness, redemption, and reconciliation that comes with the favor of the Lord.

And now, so can you!

But how do we access *this "power of the Holy Spirit?"*

Chapter 9

I Won't Back Down

"Faithfulness requires the courage to risk everything on Jesus, the willingness to keep growing, and the readiness to risk failure throughout our lives."

BRENNAN MANNING, *THE RAGAMUFFIN GOSPEL*[1]

THE MAGDALENE: STRENGTH, COURAGE, LOVE, AND GRACE

MARY MAGDALENE IS ONE of the most speculated about people in the New Testament. As early as the second century, numerous extra-biblical stories began to circulate about her. In 591 A.D., Pope Gregory preached a sermon that identified Mary Magdalene as the unnamed sinner or prostitute mentioned in Luke 7:37–38. However, there is no biblical support for this connection.

What we do know from the accounts in Matthew, Mark, Luke, and John is that Mary proved to be more loyal to Jesus than even the

1. Manning, *Ragamuffin Gospel*.

individually selected and personally trained twelve disciples. When Jesus was seized and subjected to a sham trial, His closest allies fled. Not Mary. Instead of hiding after His arrest, she stood near the cross as Jesus died. She also went to the tomb to anoint His body with spices, and she was the first to see and talk with the resurrected Jesus.

When Mary Magdalene Meets Jesus

According to biblical accounts, when Mary Magdalene first encountered Jesus, she was a mess. At that first meeting, Jesus freed Mary of seven demons. We don't know with any certainty how these demons acted themselves out in her life, but it is safe to say she struggled mightily with them. As a woman of means, she had probably sought help from many others to be free of these demons and their influence. But, until she met Jesus of Nazareth, no one else had been able to help her.

But in a moment, in a single sentence, Jesus set her free and forever changed her life. A devoted believer, she traveled with Jesus and the disciples as they ministered throughout Galilee and Judea.

Out of her personal resources, Mary helped care for Jesus and the needs of His disciples. She was deeply devoted to Jesus and stayed with Him at the foot of the cross during His crucifixion, even when others fled in fear.

Because Mary Magdalene was identified in all four gospels to be the first to share the good news of Christ's resurrection, she is often called the first evangelist. She is mentioned more often than any other woman in the New Testament.

But have you considered what it cost her to be a follower of Jesus?

Mary of Magdala certainly loved Jesus. She loved Him fiercely and stood with Him even in death. Can you imagine seeing the one you loved brutally beaten, ruthlessly ridiculed, and violently executed? Remember, the execution of Jesus was not quick or humane. It was a spectacle that played out for many hours. He was beaten, forced to carry His own cross, a crown of thorns was pounded into His skull, and nails were driven through His hands and feet and

He was hung on a cross. Then for hours, He struggled to breathe. Finally, when He had forgiven His persecutors and breathed His last, He was run through with a spear to prove He was dead.

And Mary Magdalene stood there with Him. She saw it all, but she was not done, and she did not quit. While others ran away or gave up and went home, she stood with Jesus.

While others were asleep or in hiding, she prepared the spices and went to the tomb to see that He was cared for with love and compassion. We have sanitized death today. Even when one of our loved ones dies, we don't have to deal with the gruesome details of preparing a body for burial. Mary did. She was prepared to follow Jesus all the way, even to the bloody end.

What was she thinking when she headed out for His tomb? There was a large stone rolled over the entrance to the grave. It would likely take several strong men to move that stone. And what of the Roman guards? How was she going to get past them? Finally, the grave was sealed with the imperial seal of Pilate. Anyone breaking that seal would ignite the anger of Rome and its governor.

But Mary did not hesitate.

She did not waver.

She did not flinch. She did not back down.

So great was her love and devotion she stood by Jesus to the very end and beyond.[2]

2. Car, "Real Reason Why Mary Magdalene Is Such a Controversial Figure."

MAGDALENE

I was afraid of the face
That I saw looking back
This world will break
That which it cannot understand
I was scarred I was scared Seven devils haunted me
In your love, I learned to finally
See what you saw in me
I feel holy when I'm with you
I feel whole and I feel moved
I will not waver
I will not break
I will stand by your side
Let the world come as it may
I am not afraid
Let the danger come
What will be will be
I lie my faith in you, You set me free
I will not turn away
When the darkness comes
I lie my faith in you
You alone are enough
I feel holy when I'm with you
I feel whole and I feel moved
I will not waver
I will not break
I will stand by your side
Let the world come as it may
I am not afraid
Lyrics: Richard Miller -2021

WRUNKEN: THE COURAGEOUS HOUSEMAID

Executed at 13.

During the time of the Spanish Inquisition, there was a young girl who had extraordinary faith, courage and vision. Her name was Wrunken and she was executed for refusing to renounce her faith in God and her study of the scriptures. She was only 13 years old.

This took place in the 1500's in what is now Belgium. King Philip of Spain was determined to eradicate Protestants, no matter the cost. He viewed the reading of the Bible by laymen or common people as heresy. In order to stamp out such apostasy, he sent one of his most effective military generals to Belgium. That general was the Duke of Alba. He was ruthless in his mission to destroy the Protestant heretics. Upon his arrival, he had 22 people simultaneously decapitated.

He followed the executions with a search of the city for anyone who owned a Bible. When he entered the home of the town mayor an intense interrogation was begun and in the process a Bible was discovered. When confronted with the evidence, the mayor denied that anyone in the house ever read it. The interrogation continued with the mayor's servants and when they began questioning his 13 year-old housemaid, Wrunken, she testified that it was her Bible and that she was reading it. The young girl was immediately put in chains and hauled off to prison. Wrunken refused to abandon her faith and was sentenced to death. She would be placed into a hollowed-out space inside the city wall, sealed in, brick by brick and left to suffocate.

While she awaited execution, she remained resolute in her faith. Many hoped that she would deny her faith to avoid the tortuous death. The mayor visited the girl in jail and implored her to recant. When she would not, he was so moved by her faith, that he asked her to pray for his salvation and he became a believer.

Even in these desperate moments, Wrunken's concerns were not what one would expect from a 13-year-old:

- She prayed that she would remain strong and suffer her inquisitor's questions without wavering.

- She hoped that she could endure the humiliation of being paraded through the streets of the city while being mercilessly taunted and jeered at.

- She was concerned about the mayor and his new-found faith. She prayed that he would remain strong.

- She prayed that her dream of printing Bibles and teaching the scriptures to orphaned children would go on.

When execution day arrived, she was again begged to deny her lord and savior. She refused.

She was led to the cavity in the city wall, tied up and placed in it. They began to seal over the opening. As she stood in the death chamber, an official tried to persuade her to recant saying,

"So young and beautiful—and yet to die."

Wrunken replied, "My savior died for me, I will also die for him."

Just as the last stone was being placed, she was warned again, "You will die in there!"

She replied, "I will be with Jesus."

"Just repent and you will go free!"

Wrunken's response? "Oh Lord, forgive my murderers."

She did not back down.

The last brick was set and sealed. Many years later, her bones were removed from the wall and buried in the city cemetery.

Had evil triumphed? Did this young girl perish for nothing? Did her dreams die with her? The answer is no, execution is not the end of Wrunken's story. While they could suffocate this young girl, they could not quench the Holy Spirit that lived within her.

The mayor's life had been radically transformed, not only by Wrunken's fortitude in the face of persecution, but by his new faith in Christ Jesus. His wife met a young girl named Isabella, from the same orphanage Wrunken had lived in and their hearts were stirred. The mayor and his wife adopted her.

What about Wrunken's dream of getting a printing press to print Bibles, and having a place to teach children about Jesus? The mayor developed a large, hidden, underground room with a press for the printing of Bibles. He then added a classroom in his home for the teaching of young children and he felt certain that Isabela would carry on Wrunken's dream.[3]

Where did she find the conviction and courage? She trusted in Jesus and the Holy Spirit gave her strength. She knew that her Savior deeply loved her and that this was not the end of her story.

3. This section was written based on three sources: "Jesus Freak" by DC Talk, "Wrunken the Martyr," and https://salvationstudiohouse.com/loved-not-their-lives and 3.

You have a story too. It's time to start living it to the fullest!!

"Yet, in all these things, we are more than conquerors through Him who loved us."
-Romans 8:37 NKJV

We are more than conquerors and we are more than raga-muffins. We are truly blessed, highly favored, and deeply loved.

A MATTER OF PERSPECTIVE

If you find yourself lying on a deserted beach on a tropical island oasis with cool breezes blowing and clear fresh running water at your side, where are you? Are you on a luxury vacation or are you a castaway on a remote desert island in the middle of the ocean? Perhaps for the first few days, you can view it as a vacation, a break from the rat race. It is when you realize that you are alone, have no hope of escape, no one knows where you are and that you have been given up for dead, then and only then can you really appreciate the need for rescue.

So it is with our lives. It is not until we realize that we are lost, adrift, broken, incapable, and without purpose that we can begin to see the need for rescue or the need for a savior. The need to be saved from ourselves, our sins, and our selfishness.

For all have sinned and fall short of the glory of God.
-Romans 3:23

For me, the realization of my own depravity would take years of wrestling to understand. Somewhere along the way, I conceded that many of my actions were improper, and needed to change. That realization is a necessity. Unless and until we come to know as a moral certainty that we have failed, that we have missed the mark, we cannot begin the journey to wholeness.

It is the master work of the Great Deceiver to convince us that we are on a perpetual vacation with no need of rescue. We are distracted from our true plight by all of our stuff: our opportunities, our possessions, recreations, ambitions and accomplishments. We take a long time to see through it all and to understand the hopelessness of all these pursuits and the helplessness of our condition.

But when we do. . .! Ahh! We've taken the first step toward life as it was meant to be! Return to the meaning of the word repent: "*Let God change the way you think.*" When our thinking changes, we can begin to use our gifts and passions here and now and for an eternal purpose as well.

I've seen some terrifying movies, and I've read some scary books. The stories that scare me most are the ones that seem like they could really happen.

Edgar Allen Poe wrote some pretty morbid short stories and poems like "Murders in the Rue Morgue," "The Tell-Tale Heart," "The Raven," and the "Masque of the Red Death." All of them are creepy and you shouldn't read them before going to bed.

But by far the most chilling poem I've ever read is "Invictus," written in 1875 by W. E. Henley:

Invictus

Out of the night that covers me,
Black as the pit from pole to pole,
I thank whatever gods may be
For my unconquerable soul.
In the fell clutch of circumstance I
have not winced nor cried aloud.
Under the bludgeoning's of chance
My head is bloody, but unbowed.
Beyond this place of wrath and tears
Looms but the Horror of the shade,
And yet the menace of the years
Finds and shall find me unafraid.
It matters not how strait the gate,
How charged with punishments the scroll,
I am the master of my fate,
I am the captain of my soul.[4]

Why is it so scary?

4. Henley, "Invictus."

It scares me because, in some ways, Henley is describing me. I often wear my own pigheadedness as a badge of honor.

Sometimes I value my "unconquerable soul" as the most crucial aspect of my identity; the idea that no matter what, I refuse to bend a knee to anyone, even a higher power.

The harder the task, the greater the obstacle; the more severe the pain, the better. I have taken pride in the doing and in the overcoming. I may have been bloodied in the process, but I have refused to yield.

Years ago, I undertook a particularly grueling challenge that imposed intense physical and mental stress. It came in the form of a dare or a bet. It was extreme. At one point, my partner in the undertaking felt that he couldn't take it anymore. He said that he might turn back, that he might quit. It was too hard, too dangerous.

He was probably correct in his analysis of the situation. We should have quit. We were putting our lives at risk over a stupid bet.

My response?

"You can turn back if you want to, but I will die out here before I stop. I will not give them the satisfaction of seeing me quit."

What a blockhead!

I am the master of my fate; I am the captain of my soul. Really? Me, the master of my fate? The captain of my soul? If that is the case, then I am indeed lost.

Would you get on a bus that had a blind bus driver? Board a plane captained by a pilot who'd never flown before?

Reality check.

The certainty here is that I am neither master of my fate nor the captain of my soul.

Yes, I have "free will," but even that is held captive by my broken nature.

> *"I do not understand what I do. For what I want to do, I do not do, but what I hate, I do."* Romans 7:15 NIV

I am either enslaved by my own lusts and perceptions or set free by the love of Jesus.

But even set free, I am not completely released from this broken psyche. While I will advance and grow in faith, hope, and love, in this life I will never be absolutely free from the malfunctions of spirit inherited with my depraved nature.

Sound grim, seem hopeless?

On the contrary, that brokenness, the self-inflicted wounds, overblown self-image, and pigheaded pride provide a perfect context or background for the unconditional love of Jesus to be revealed.

He loved me enough to pursue me.

He pursued me through my sin, pain, pride and stubbornness. He allowed me to do all of the stupid things that I did, so at the end of the day, I would know two truths without any shadow of a doubt.

The two truths?

First, I am capable of doing really dumb things and incapable of even doing really good things for the right reasons.

Second, He loves me enough to pursue me through the sewer of my depravity, to the very peaks of my arrogance, and even into the valley of death because He loves me as I am, not as I should be.

Did you hear that?

> "He loves me as I am, not as I should be."
> —Brennan Manning

We are not alone, and I am not the first fool to think that I could control my world and bend it to my own will and desires. Take a look at the story of Jacob and Esau. The brothers were the grandsons of Abraham.

From birth, Jacob was determined to get his own way. He was born just seconds after his brother, Esau, so he was the younger brother. However, as if to make a statement of his refusal to accept second place, Jacob exited the womb clutching his brother by the heel.

He made a career out of getting his way at any cost: trickery, deception, manipulation, whatever it took to get the job done. And all the while he was winning, he was getting richer. He came to believe that his prosperity was due to his superior intellect, wit, and strategic thinking.

We often view the account in Genesis 32 in which Jacob wrestles all night with an angel as one of noble strength or persistence on Jacob's part. He grappled with the holy messenger into the early morning hours and would not let him go. As the sun rose, the angel said to Jacob,

"Let me go."

But Jacob refused.

Jacob's reply? *"I will not let you go unless you bless me."*

Sometimes we are told that Jacob made this demand because he had overcome or overpowered the celestial being.

Both my research and my life experience tell me something very different.

After an all-night struggle, the angel touched Jacob's hip and disabled him. At that moment, Jacob realized the wrestling match he had engaged in for so many hours was futile. The supernatural being could have debilitated him at any point in the contest and could continue to disable him if he so desired.

After contending in his own strength throughout the night, it dawned on Jacob when the angel touched his hip that, in and of himself, his toughness was nothing compared to the power of the celestial being with whom he had spent all night wrestling. It is in the context of this realization that Jacob makes his demand,

"I will not let go until you bless me."

Jacob makes the demand, not as a victor who has prevailed over his foe. Rather, he blurts out this last ultimatum to declare:

"I have nothing left. With the coming of the new day, I will die at the hand of the brother I have cheated. I will not let you go because I cannot let you go. If you will not bless me, protect me, or come to my aid, I might as well be dead.

You can kill me now or you can bless me, but I'm not letting go."

Jacob had come to a crossroad—a seminal moment and the dawning of a new reality.

All of his life, from birth to that very day, Jacob had succeeded in achieving his goals by scheming, plotting, strategizing, and taking advantage of others.

He took pride in all that he had accomplished and amassed as testimony to his supremacy. He was convinced of his own superiority. It had served him well his entire life. But now, with all the chips on the table and the last cards dealt, Jacob realized he was holding a losing hand.

All of his life, he had bet on the wrong player. Now, faced with the biggest wager of his life, he couldn't bluff or call. He was out of chips with nowhere to run.

Finally, Jacob has crossed over from scheming his way through life by power and wit to a new reality.

He is slapped in the face. He comes to realize and accept that he was nothing without God's blessing. He understands for the first time that all that he had gained, the riches he had amassed, were not going to save him. All he had accomplished was worthless when it came to acquiring the favor of God.

He was finished.

Nothing left.

Done.

He was broken.

Out of resources, out of strategies, out of time.

In the course of my spiritual journey, I had to get to a place where I had nothing left of my own resources to pull me through. I had done everything that I could think of to meet God's conditions. I exerted my will and self-discipline to avoid repeating mistakes and failures. I worked overtime to "do good" until finally, I came to the end of myself. As the captain of my soul, I had driven my life onto the rocks.

I was broken.

Out of resources, out of strategies, out of time.

I was finished.

Nothing left.

Done.

But when I was done, Jesus was there, arms outstretched and full of love.

His soul spoke quietly to mine:

"If you're finished trying to do this on your own, then lean on me. Trust me. Love me.

Together, you and I can change the world."

How about you?

Are you done yet?

With a new perspective on my human condition, I recently penned a response to William Henley's "Invictus" titled "Liberatus."

LIBERATUS

Into the flame that quickens me
A rage like fire does drive me still
I thank whatever fates may be
For the freedom of my will

The pound of flesh I gladly paid
In order that I stake my claim
To seize the prize, my just reward
Yet only smoke and grief remain

But on that mound of toil and tears
Blood like grace and mercy spilled
A phoenix from the ash did rise
To be all that destiny has willed

The fires of life meld love and loss
To forge at last a perfect whole
I bow to the author of my fate
I bless the lover of my soul

-Richard Avery Miller

Chapter 10

A Brand New Day

"The litmus test of our love for God is our love of neighbor."
BRENNAN MANNING, *THE WISDOM OF TENDERNESS*[1]

THE TIME IS NOW

THE IDEA OF THIS brave new world can be both inspiring and overwhelming. How can we contribute to this new kingdom? Is it too big? Where do we start?

We begin by clarifying the good news of the gospel and that clarification starts with addressing misinformation about the message that Jesus, our friend and redeemer, taught.

We celebrate the unmerited grace and mercy of God who forgives all our sins and heals our diseases. But we are more than just rescued and redeemed ragamuffins or vagabonds. We were, after all, created in the very image of God.

1. Manning, *Wisdom of Tenderness*.

Through the life, death, and resurrection of Jesus, we have been grafted into the family of God, Jehovah, the most powerful being in the cosmos. In fact, He is the creator and sustainer of this ever expanding and evolving universe.

As the creator and ultimate artist, He has authority over this world that He created. Our adoption into the family of God and the ongoing redemption of our personal brokenness is a beginning. From there we can step into fellowship with the Holy Spirit and begin to synchronize our gifts and passions with His. Our talents and idiosyncrasies have been built into our very DNA. With the help of the Spirit of God, we can now fully deploy those talents. We are free now to experience that which has been our destiny since before we were born.

We may not be the center of the universe, but our work is essential in the building of the Kingdom of God. Engaging our world with our God-given talents and passions is part of the ongoing story of redemption and reconciliation.

These gifts and passions are a representation of our perfect Heavenly Father's attributes, an expression of our individual destinies, and a foreshadowing of our commission within the everlasting, ever growing Kingdom of God.

There is coming a day when our perfection is realized, our brokenness healed, our enemy is vanquished, and we are free!

Free to do what? Free to participate in the eternal process of exploring, building and maintaining all expects of this universe and the Kingdom of Heaven, in partnership with Jesus.

Our gifts will be strengthened by the Spirit of God and together we will create an unstoppable eternal force for good. We will live in a kingdom, guided by the Holy Spirit, and governed by love, forever.

Psalm 23

A psalm of David.
The Lord is my shepherd, I lack nothing.
He makes me lie down in green pastures,
He leads me beside quiet waters,
He refreshes my soul.
He guides me along the right paths
For his names' sake.
Even though I walk
through the darkest valley,
I will fear no evil,
For you are with me;
your rod and your staff,
they comfort me.
You prepare a table before me
in the presence of my enemies.
You anoint my head with oil;
my cup overflows.
surely your goodness and love will follow me
all the days of my life,
and I will dwell in the house of the Lord,
forever (NIV)

FULL ARMOR

> *Finally, my brethren, be strong in the Lord, and in the power of his might. Put on the whole armor of God, that ye may be able to stand against the wiles of the devil.*
>
> *For we wrestle not against flesh and blood, but against principalities, against powers, against the rulers of the darkness of this world, against spiritual wickedness in high places.*
>
> *Wherefore take unto you the whole armor of God, that ye may be able to withstand in the evil day, and having done all, to stand.*
>
> *Stand therefore, having your loins girt about with truth, and having on the breastplate of righteousness;*
>
> *And your feet shod with the preparation of the gospel of peace;*
>
> *Above all, taking the shield of faith, wherewith ye shall be able to quench all the fiery darts of the wicked.*
>
> *And take the helmet of salvation, and the sword of the Spirit, which is the word of God:*
>
> *Praying always with all prayer and supplication in the Spirit, and watching thereunto with all perseverance and supplication for all saints.* -Ephesians 6:10–19 KJV

Finally, brothers and sisters, remember that we are in a fight. The Great Liar is running hard to defeat and destroy all that God loves, especially you and me. The apostle Paul reminds us that God has provided us with protections and the weapons of war in this spiritual confrontation. He calls upon us to put on the *"whole armor of God"* so that we might be able to stand against the schemes of the devil.

Paul isn't just using metaphor or writing poetry about some ethereal universe. If we are going to go to war with the evil forces of the world, we must literally use all the weapons at our disposal. Every day we must rise up and prepare for the battle ahead.

Strap on the breastplate of righteousness, being confident of the righteousness of Jesus imputed to us. Tighten the belt of His truth around your waist by diving into God's word. Stay connected with our commander in chief through constant prayer.

Pick up your shield of faith—the faith you have in Jesus—and step into the fray. Remember that this faith that protects you comes from the trust you have in Him and the evidence of His work on your behalf. Evidence that you can see in your own life as well as the evidence presented by sinners turned saints throughout history and up to this very day.

Remind yourself every day that He paid the price for your ransom. The surety of your salvation is a helmet that will protect you and see you through, so put it on!

Lace up your boots and prepare to share the story of God's goodness, love, and peace. It's not going to be tiptoeing through the tulips, it's going to be a brawl.

Finally, arm yourself with the sword of the Spirit of God. We are not meant to be helpless punching bags for evil forces to pummel, passively taking the beatings that they want to dish out. We are called to be warriors, bold and courageous for our King and His kingdom; for our sons and daughters, for our friends and family, and for the helpless and exploited people of this world.

Make no mistake, there will be bloodshed in this struggle. Be dauntless in the face of darkness. The mighty God of the universe has your back.

And we are assured of this—He wins.

God wins.

Love wins and in Him we win.

Are you ready for combat?

EMPOWERED BY GRACE

We are destined to build the Kingdom of God with Jesus as our foundation, the Holy Spirit as our helper, God's own words as our guide, and love as our fuel.

In our present state, you and I are flawed human beings. Yes, we were created in the very image of God, but when sin entered the picture, we became imperfect in our being. We are imperfect in our thoughts, actions, and the way we speak with each other.

When we read the story of Adam and Eve in the book of Genesis, we see that once they had disobeyed God, they tried to cover their nakedness.

THE FALL

Going back to Genesis 3

> . . .she took of its fruit and ate, and she also gave some to her husband who was with her, and he ate. Then the eyes of both were opened, and they knew that they were naked. And they sewed fig leaves together and made themselves loincloths. And they heard the sound of the Lord God walking in the garden in the cool of the evening, and the man and his wife hid themselves from the presence of the Lord God among the tress of the garden. But the Lord God called to the man and said to him, "Where are you?" And he said, "I heard the sound of you in the garden, and I was afraid, because I was naked, and I hid myself." He said, "Who told you that you were naked? Have you eaten of the tree of which I commanded you not to eat?" The man said, "The woman whom you gave to be with me, she gave me fruit of the tree, and I ate." Then the Lord God said to the woman, "What is this that you have done?" The woman said, "The serpent deceived me, and I ate."

God said to them," *Well, who told you that you were naked?"* The answer? No one. No one had to tell them as their sin made them self-aware: aware of their nakedness. It made them aware of good as well as evil.

But it did more than make them self-aware. It made them self-centered; selfish in their words and deeds and that selfishness has been passed down through every generation since.

Okay, so what do we do now? Just shrug our shoulders and say, *"Hey, well I inherited this selfish nature and there's not much I can do about it, so I'll just live with it and hope I don't hurt too many people along the way."*

No.

I believe there is a better, more proactive alternative. While it is true that we will never reach complete holiness or perfection in this life, we can begin the process of moving toward becoming the people that God originally intended us to be.

BETTER THAN PERFECT

I am the proud grandfather of beautiful and amazing grandkids. In fact, those children may be the cutest kids in the whole world! They are each awesome in their own way.

Are they perfect?

My heart tells me yes, but my theology tells me no.

In fact, I believe they may be better than perfect.

"Can we be perfect?"

This question came up in a Bible study group that I am a part of. The group's consensus that night was "No, nobody's perfect." However, consensus does not necessarily mean unanimous consent.

It was suggested that perhaps there is more than one right answer to that question.

So, is it possible to be perfect?

Well, maybe.

It depends on what you mean by perfect.

I learned some time ago, when studying the rules of debate, that one foundational strategy of any good argument is defining the vocabulary of the debate. Whoever establishes the definitions of key vocabulary terms used in the dispute will usually win.

So, let's define our term.

How does the dictionary define "perfect?"

a: being without fault or defect

But "perfect" does not have to mean flawless, without blemish, spotless or new, never used, no dents, dings or scratches. Actually, there are several definitions for the word.

b: satisfies all requirements

c: completely suited for a particular purpose or situation

Why stop at perfect? As long as I'm pushing the boundaries, let me ask another question.

Is there something or someone that is better than perfect?

The Japanese have a concept that may help explain "better than perfect." The term WABI does not translate very well into English but is helpful as a concept within the framework of a worldview. Essentially, it is the idea of finding beauty in imperfection.

My dad was a research chemist. He was logical and analytical. He worked on top-secret government projects and had a number of talents.

Woodworking, however, was not one of them.

When he retired from the defense industry, he bought some tools to put in his shop with the idea of becoming a woodworker. He made a few pieces, bookends and candlesticks, and a few other items. But none of them were very good. Some were a little lopsided or didn't stand up straight or wouldn't hold a candle.

But do you want to know something? I inherited some of his bookends, and every time I see them, I smile. Sure, they are a little wonky, but that's why I enjoy them so much. They remind me of my dad. There is beauty in imperfection. To me, these pieces are better because they are not flawless. They are "better than perfect."

You may say something like, "See, he's already conceded the argument by admitting to imperfection."

However, I'll say, "Not so fast. Stick with me for a minute or two. We're not done yet."

We now have two questions; "Can we be perfect?" and "Is there perfection within imperfection itself?"

Back to our definition:

a: being without fault or defect

If you have studied how to take multiple-choice tests like the SAT, you will know that

a.) Isn't always the right answer.

I'll ask you to consider definitions b, c, d, e and f.

b: Satisfies all requirements

c: Completely suited for a particular purpose or situation

d: fulfills the intended purpose, performs as intended

e: Hit the sweet spot, found the "perfect pitch"

f: Is exactly what I need, when I need it.

Are b, c, d, e, and f acceptable definitions of "perfect?" I think, in the right context, even Noah Webster would agree that they are.

THE PERFECT GAME

A "perfect game" in baseball does not mean 27 batters, 81 pitches, all strikes, no balls, no-fly balls or ground balls. No, a perfect game means no batter reaching base for any reason; no runs, no walks, no hits, no errors. A batter may hit the ball well, but he gets put out by a miraculous catch in the outfield or an extraordinary play in the infield. So, although the pitcher was not perfect, he played his role in creating a perfect game.

How about a perfect season in football? Does it mean not allowing any opponent any yardage in any game or not allowing an opponent to score in any game? No, it means that a team won every game played that season.

While you think about that, let me pose some questions:

Which would you choose:

You are preparing for a state championship baseball game—one game to decide it all. Your whole season comes down to just one contest. You have to select the glove that you are going to use in the game. Which one will you choose? A brand-spankin' new glove right off the shelf of your favorite sporting goods store? No nicks, scratches, scuffs or flaws?

-or-

Do you go with the glove that you have used for the past four years? The glove that is broken in, well oiled, dinged up, scuffed up, and fits your hand perfectly? I don't know about you, but I'm using the one that fits perfectly for me. The one that is smeared with years of sweat and oil and dirt, but also has a perfect "pocket" that I know will hold the ball that I'm trying to catch.

Okay, so you've never played baseball, let's talk about jeans. Which pair of jeans would be "perfect" for you? Brand new Levi's right off the shelf, stiff, dark blue, never been worn, never washed and never stained?

-or-

Do you choose the pair that "fits just right?" Your favorite pair of jeans, a little worn, a little faded, maybe with a frayed hem or a rip at the knee; the pair of jeans that not only "fits just right" but that also has a story that goes along with them?

So, you don't like baseball and you don't wear blue jeans. Let's talk cooking. A cast-iron frying pan. Which one do you choose? The one direct from the foundry, never used, never touched by a speck of food or a dab of oil?

-or-

Will you select the one that is "seasoned?" The one with a patina and has been in your family for years: heated up, cooled down with the DNA of grandma's favorite dishes cooked into the very pores of the skillet?

Let's get back to the questions: Is it possible to be perfect? How about better than perfect?

My answer to both questions is,

Yes, absolutely!

So, how can we be perfect?

Perfection comes as we fulfill the function for which we were designed. And what were we designed for? Floating on a cloud and strumming a harp? Or was it to be about our Heavenly Father's business? The business of stewarding His creation? The organizational process of naming all living things? The joy found in His directive to "be fruitful and multiply" and the pleasure of walking and talking with God in the cool of the evening?

In short, managing God's creation in partnership with God Himself.

Not independent from Him.

Not distanced from Him.

With Him. Simultaneously for our joy and for His Glory.

Here it is: God knew us before we were born, before we were conceived and before we were even a twinkle in our daddy's eye.

Ephesians chapter 2:10 tells us:

> *"In Christ Jesus, God made us new people so that we would spend our lives doing the good things he had already planned for us to do."* (ESV)

The great work of building the Kingdom of Heaven, hand in hand, with God's Holy Spirit.

One day at a time. One act of love at a time.

> *"Now, these three remain: faith, hope, and love, and the greatest of these is love."*
> I Corinthians 13:13 NIV

Not only were we designed for a purpose, when we step into a living, loving, active relationship with God through Christ Jesus, we are then outfitted with all the tools we need to fulfill our purpose. Love, joy, peace, patience, gentleness, goodness, meekness, and self-control. God imprinted into our DNA specific characteristics, interests, and passions. The fall of man contributed flaws, blemishes, and even disabilities. But we were created with strengths, weaknesses, gifts, and talents for a specific purpose. In and through Him, the weak are made strong, sinners made saints and rebels turned righteous. The last are first and the dead are made to live again.

Each day I see my students doing the things God has purposed for them to do; in the hallways, as volunteers at the soup kitchen, and on the playing field. When I see a 16-year-old high school football player kneeling in front of an 86-year-old resident of a skilled nursing facility speaking, listening, laughing, praying, sharing life, I believe that in that moment, they are doing what God designed them to do. It is in that sense, at that moment, they are perfect.

When a shy 15-year-old high school sophomore shares life with the disadvantaged, living out acts of compassion and love, with absolutely no expectation of reciprocity, no quid pro quo, no intent to pad a college resume, just a heart ready to share moments of life and love, in that moment of active love, I see perfection. When I see believers interacting in love with the marginalized and downtrodden, in that instant, in that conversation, in that prayer, in that laughter, I see hints of God. I see perfection.

The well-worn baseball glove that is a perfect fit to the hand that grasps it, precisely formed to the hand that shaped it, perfectly suited for its intended purpose, is a greater expression of perfection than the one off the shelf brand new. It is because of the rough work of playing the game, because of the shape of the well-worn pocket that it is ideally suited for its purpose. It may not be pretty to look at, but the "imperfections" make the well-used tool the ideal choice because of its history, rough edges and because it performs exactly as intended. It is the perfect tool with which to play the game.

And so it is with us. We may be scuffed, worn, beaten, bruised, and not much to look at, but the experience that we own because of our individual journeys makes us perfectly suited for God's purpose. The potholes and rough spots in your pilgrimage to the Father make you who you are and fit you for service far better than a smooth road lined with daffodils and daisies.

We have been perfectly prepared to live out our destiny, to do that for which we were created. To love, to share, to speak, to listen, to lead, to laugh, and to cry. And as we do what we were designed and equipped to do, we find our groove.

You and I, bumped and bruised, refined in the fires of life, operating in cooperation with the Spirit of God Himself, and empowered by His love, find our destinies. Faint glimpses of selflessness. Hints of faith, hope, and love.

Fleeting previews of who we can be!

It is in those moments that we are, yes, perfect.

PERFECTION AT THE PLATE

In Brooklyn, New York, Chush is a school that caters to learning disabled children. Some children remain in Chush for their entire school career, while others can be mainstreamed into conventional schools.

At a fund-raising dinner, the father of a disabled child delivered a speech that will never be forgotten by all who attended.

After extolling the school and its dedicated staff, he cried out, "Where is the perfection in my son Shaya? Everything God does is done with perfection. But my child cannot understand things as other children do. My child cannot remember facts and figures as other children do. Where is God's perfection?"

The audience was shocked by the question, pained by the father's anguish, stilled by the piercing query.

"I believe," the father answered, "that when God brings a child like this into the world, the perfection that He seeks is in the way people react to this child."

He then told the following story about his son, Shaya:

One afternoon, Shaya and his father walked past a park where some boys Shaya knew were playing baseball.

Shaya asked, "Do you think they will let me play?"

Shaya's father knew that his son was not at all athletic and that most boys would not want him on their team. But Shaya's father understood that if his son was chosen to play, it would give him a comfortable sense of belonging.

Shaya's father approached one of the boys in the field and asked if Shaya could play. The boy looked around for guidance from his teammates. Getting none, he took matters into his own hands and said, "We are losing by six runs and the game is in the eighth inning. I guess he can be on our team, and we'll try to put him up to bat in the ninth inning." Shaya's father was ecstatic as Shaya smiled broadly. Shaya was told to put on a glove and go out to play short center field.

In the bottom of the eighth inning, Shaya's team scored a few runs but was still behind by three. In the bottom of the ninth inning, Shaya's team scored again, and now with two outs and the bases loaded with the potential winning run on base, Shaya was scheduled to be the next batter. Would the team actually let Shaya bat at this juncture and give away their chance to win the game? Surprisingly, Shaya was given the bat.

Everyone knew that it was all but impossible because Shaya didn't even know how to hold the bat properly, let alone hit with it. However, as Shaya stepped up to the plate, the pitcher moved a few steps closer to lob the ball in softly, so Shaya should at least be able to make contact.

The first pitch came in, and Shaya swung clumsily and missed. One of Shaya's teammates came up to Shaya and together they held the bat then faced the pitcher, waiting for the next pitch. The pitcher again took a few steps forward to toss the ball softly toward Shaya. As the pitch came in, Shaya and his teammate swung the bat, and together they hit a slow ground ball to the pitcher.

The pitcher picked up the soft grounder and could easily have thrown the ball to the first baseman. Shaya would have been out, and that would have ended the game. Instead, the pitcher took the ball and threw it on a high arc to right field, far beyond the reach of the first baseman.

Everyone started yelling, "Shaya, run to first! Run to first!" Never in his life had Shaya run to first. He scampered down the baseline wide-eyed and startled. By the time he reached first base, the right fielder had the ball. He could have thrown the ball to the second baseman, who would tag out Shaya, who was still running. But the right fielder understood what the pitcher's intentions were, so he threw the ball high and far over the third baseman's head. Everyone yelled, "Run to second, run to second!" Shaya ran towards second base as the runners ahead of him deliriously circled the bases towards home. As Shaya reached second base, the opposing shortstop ran to him, turned him in the direction of third base, and shouted, "Run to third!" As Shaya rounded third, the boys from both teams ran behind him, screaming, "Shaya, run home!"

Shaya ran home, stepped on home plate, and all eighteen boys lifted him on their shoulders and made him the hero, as he had just hit a grand slam and won the game for his team!

"That day," said the father softly with tears now rolling down his face, "those eighteen boys reached a type of God's perfection."[2]

SO WHAT?

So, what's the point?

To convince you of the possibility of sinless perfection? No.

The point is to suggest that each of us is a part of God's story, part of His kingdom and that we have work to do. The point is to remind each of us that because of the life and death and resurrection of Jesus Christ, God the Father sees you and me as perfect.

God does not hold our sin against us.

In the blood of Jesus, all our sin stains are gone, and we have been washed as white as snow.

The point is to encourage you to leave your baggage behind.

To entreat you to quit dragging your burden of shame and guilt along with you.

To challenge you to remember that God says that you are *"fearfully and wonderfully made."*

To call you to accept Jesus' offer of forgiveness and love. To enjoy the relief in knowing that you are always in His thoughts, always on his mind.

To convince you that you are loved and forgiven and perfect in the eyes of God.

To remind you that the work of God is right here in front of you.

To share with you that we don't have to wait until heaven to enjoy the love and grace of God or to live in the reality of His kingdom.

2. Krohn, *Perfection at the Plate.*

It is here.

It is now.

To beg you not to disqualify yourself from the race before it even starts because your focus is on your guilt instead of His glory.

To assure you that His yoke is easy and His burden is light.

My father used to say, "You can never be faultless, but you can be blameless." That concept baffled me for years. But as I've continued on this journey that we call life I can see what he meant. I think what he was trying to say was that you are never going to be 100% correct in your words and actions. Mistakes and mishaps happen all the time; whether through lack of information, poor understanding of the best way of doing something, or just a plain misunderstanding of the issue at hand. We will never be completely faultless or error free. For that matter, even computers have programming issues, bad code or corrupted files, and so do we.

But when it comes to being blameless, we can work toward doing whatever our tasks are with the proper motive and a pure heart. We can do our best to do what is right and treat others with fairness and respect. To live and speak and act with integrity. When we find we've missed the mark, we must confess it, do our best to make it right, ask forgiveness and move forward. We should do this with the aid and comfort of the Holy Spirit.

Here's a personal example. In my role as a high school principal, I dealt with plenty of issues. With hundreds of people, both students and teachers under my care, difficulties arose every day. On one of those days a teacher of ninth grade students called down to the office in tears because some unruly students were being rude and disrespectful. She was frustrated and at her wits end. She called the office for help.

It was a busy day for me, with lots of meetings, deadlines, reports, and reviews, and this was not the first time I'd had to deal with this same group of rowdies. Upon hearing from that teacher, I was fired up. I stormed down to that classroom and lit those kids up. I said something to the effect of ". . . I've had it with you guys! Enough is enough! If you can't get your act together and show your teachers some respect, you're gonna' be out of here! I don't care if you come to school here or not!"

The room was deadly quiet. I left the room and stomped back to my office.

The next morning, I got a call from a parent of one of the ninth-grade culprits. She said her son came home after school and told her the story, and she repeated what her son told her I had said. She asked, "Did you really say that?" Unfortunately, I had to confirm her son's story. I knew I had messed up, and I had to make it right.

I walked down to the same classroom, same period, same teacher, and same students. When I walked in the door, it got really quiet. Those kids were bracing for another tongue-lashing.

"Ok guys, when you make a mistake, when you mess up, I call you out and hold you accountable. Yesterday, I chewed you out, and I said some things I shouldn't have said. If I'm going to hold you accountable, then I have to be accountable as well. With that said, I'm here to apologize and to ask your forgiveness. I tore you up in public so now I must apologize publicly. I'm sorry, and I hope you can forgive me."

The students' faces softened, and the tension that had been in that room disappeared.

Let me tell you something. That group of freshmen had something of a reputation for causing trouble, but after that incident, and after my apology, I didn't have a problem with any of those kids for the rest of the school year. Was it fun to apologize and attempt to make things right? No. Could I have justified my actions by saying that those students got what they deserved? Sure. If they had not been disrespectful in the first place none of this would have happened. But even though they had it coming, it was not okay for me to unleash my anger on a group of kids.

You see, none of us are faultless. We must do our best and make things right when we get it wrong, and then keep moving ahead with the work we are called to.

While I understand now what my dad meant, it still isn't an easy thing to do. I'm still an imperfect person. I still have selfishness as a part of my make-up. I still fall back into being self-centered and end up hurting others in the process.

So, is there a solution to this self-centeredness that will help us move the needle closer to being blameless in our speech and actions?

The good news is, yes there is. And the remedy is simple. But, be advised, simple does not mean easy.

ANYTHING BUT ORDINARY

Families develop rules and customs over time and often these are passed on from one generation to another. Even before my dad became a Christian, there seemed to be two rules in our home while we were growing up:

- Do the right thing.
- Tell the truth.

Simple, but not natural. Not always convenient. Not easy.

As I raised my own children, I had the same expectations for them. Do the right thing, and tell the truth.

In addition, when I talked with my kids about what it takes to be successful in life, I tried to make that simple as well.

- Get up. Show up. Do the best you can.
- Try to love the people God puts in your path today.

Get up and go to work. One day at a time, each week, each month and each year. As you do, you will eventually begin to see the fruits of your labor. Not overnight, but over time.

The Christian journey is similar. Our path is one we walk one day at a time. It's not a sprint but a marathon. But, as we make this journey, there are things we can do to recharge our spiritual batteries and strengthen our spirit. Habits that we can develop which lead to spiritual strength and health. Repeated actions that help move us toward being the lights of the world that Christ calls us to be—people of integrity who speak the truth in love and who stand fast when the storms of life arise.

In church history, these practices are referred to as the "ordinary means of grace."

As we partake in these seemingly ordinary actions, we receive new strength from the Holy Spirit. There is an element of mystery, however. What is the mystery? It lies in the additional "leverage" added by the power of the Holy Spirit within us.

A truth we must face is that we will never be perfect until we receive our glorified bodies. It is true that God gives us new, vibrant hearts when we come to know Him, but we still must deal with the sinful inclinations that come from our fallen natures. Those tendencies may cause us to doubt the goodness of God and His promises when hard times come. At those times, we can cry out to God and ask Him to overcome our doubts and fears—to give us strength to believe.

Look, for example, at the miraculous healing of the young child who was tormented by evil spirits and torn by seizures. The child's father came to Jesus, desperate for help—for a miracle—and Jesus responded in mercy.

> *"Jesus said unto him, "If thou canst believe, all things are possible to him that believeth." And straightway, the father of the child cried out, and said with tears,*
> *'Lord, I believe; help thou mine unbelief.'*
> *When Jesus saw that the people came running together, he rebuked the foul spirit, saying unto him, 'Thou dumb and deaf spirit, I charge thee, come out of him, and enter no more into him.'*
> *And the spirit cried, and rent him sore, and came out of him: and he was as one dead; insomuch that many said, He is dead.'*
> *But Jesus took the child by the hand and lifted him up; and he arose."*
> -Mark 9:23–27 KJV

The words of that desperate father resonate deep within my soul, *"Lord, I believe, help thou my unbelief."*

God knows us even better than we know ourselves. In His grace and wisdom, He has provided ways for our faith in Him and His goodness to be fortified: the ordinary means of grace. These observations and disciplines are not complex or complicated. They are the means of providing us what we need to reinforce our trust in Him. To casual observers, they don't seem special at all. They make use of common, everyday things like bread, wine, water and human speech. But combined with faith and the intentional work of the Holy Spirit, these common elements produce uncommon results. They nourish our trust in Jesus as our savior and strengthen our spirit to turn away from sin and to run to Him for mercy.

What are these ordinary means of grace?

- Prayer
- Bible reading and study
- Fellowship and community
- The Word of God preached
- The sacraments: Communion and Baptism

But these "ordinary means of grace" are anything but ordinary. These practices are packed with a power provided by the Holy Spirit.

When we practice and observe these means of grace, 2+2 does not equal 4. It is not a zero-sum game. When the Holy Spirit gets involved, His grace flows. Exponentially.

Is it 2+2=5? Or 2+2=55? I don't know what the exponent is. I can only tell you that He is at work in us, through our obedience.

Each time we pray, we have an intercessor in the person of Jesus who sits on the Father's right hand making a case for us.

Each time we read the Word of God, it awakens our understanding of God and of our role in His kingdom.

Each time we hear the Word of God preached, the Spirit of God delivers His message to our hearts, souls, and minds.

Each time we gather with fellow believers, we gather strength and encouragement from our shared experiences, and we know we do not walk this spiritual path alone. It is more than just a pep rally to rev up our energies to step back into the race. Christian fellowship is enhanced by the work of the Holy Spirit within us.

> *"Where two or three gather together in my name, there am I with them."* Matthew 18:20 NIV

Communion is more than just a remembrance or a memorial. The act of honoring Christ by symbolically partaking of His body in the bread and of His blood in the wine both confirms and energizes our walk with God. That raw, new energy comes directly from The Holy Spirit.

Baptism is more than just a passive memorial or declaration. As we partake in the baptism of another, we make a commitment to walk alongside that fellow believer as they undertake their spiritual journey. To support them, pray for them, and encourage them.

Each time we engage in these practices, the Spirit of God within us empowers us to move forward toward blamelessly building the Kingdom of God.

The Kingdom of Heaven here on earth.

Here.

Today.

Now.

From where does this new source of power flow? From the Holy Spirit Himself. How do we access this power? Through obedience and by observing these ordinary means of grace.

How much power do we get? That, my friends, is a mystery of grace.

NO SHORTCUTS

On a purely human level, our task as believers is simple. We show up day after day, week after week, year after year, and faithfully practice His ordinary means of grace. As we do, we join our great God as He builds His church in a way the world, with all its technologies and traditions, will never be able to explain.

In Exodus chapter 16 we read of God's mysterious provision of a type of bread called *manna* for the Israelites. God provided manna in the wilderness for them, but they still had to collect that manna each day to meet their physical need for nourishment. They could not collect it and store it away for future use. Neither could they only partake of the manna once and be sustained for the remainder of their journey.

As individual believers we are responsible to seek out the grace of God for our spiritual nourishment. We can't hoard grace away for future use and we can't only seek His grace once in a while. We must live and learn and grow day by day as we seek out His love, joy, mercy, and grace on a consistent basis. The ordinary means of grace are essential to a healthy, vibrant spiritual journey.

> "Jesus then said to them, "Truly, truly, I say to you, it is not Moses who has given you the bread out of heaven, but it is My Father who gives you the true bread out of heaven. For the bread of God is that which comes down out of heaven and gives life to the world." Then they said to Him, 'Lord, always give us this bread.' Jesus said to them, "I am the bread of life; he who comes to Me will not hunger, and he who believes in Me will never thirst."
> -John 6:32–35 NASB

Ligonier Ministries shares this wisdom:

> Preaching is not a powerless human explanation of the biblical text, for the Spirit accompanies it so that God's Word achieves its purposes. Prayer is more than empty words; it establishes communion between us and the Creator, thereby empowering us for belief and faithful, effective service. Baptism and the Lord's Supper are not mere memorials that we do simply because Jesus tells us to do them; rather, we participate mysteriously in Christ Himself when by faith we take part in these ordinances.

They bless us as we receive them in faith, and if we neglect them, we weaken our trust in God's work.

> The sacraments are mysteries, in that we cannot explain fully what God accomplishes through them. We do know, however, that they are more than memorial observations.

They become effectual means of grace to those with faith by the working of the Holy Spirit.[3]

THE HEALING POWER OF GRACE

*"Oh, Lord my God, I cried to you for help and you healed me." -*Psalm 30:2

Don't miss this key point. Yes, the ordinary means of grace provide the substance we need to strengthen our spiritual selves, helping us to be stronger, more informed believers and effective members of God's kingdom, but that is not all that the Holy Spirit can do as we observe these practices. These means of grace have a healing effect as well.

A truth we must face is that we all have some aspects of brokenness. Broken in spirit, emotionally scarred. We inherited our sinful nature from Adam, and we've added our own mistakes and misdeeds to the pile. Healing is something that every human being needs, to one degree or another, for we have all been wounded.

There are many types of brokenness and pain because each of our stories are unique. Sometimes our wounds are the result of another person's sin and at other times our wounds are self-inflicted. Whatever the cause, each of us fight some type of emotional or spiritual battle.

What are your areas of brokenness? As for me, I have a lengthy list of fractured puzzle pieces: I can be intense and get angry when someone interrupts my quest to finish something. At times I am guilty of trying to impress others when I should be working to glorify God. If I'm not careful I talk too much or fail to listen to what a person is saying. I often procrastinate. Sometimes I make snap judgements about other people, behave selfishly, jump from one project to another, and at times my temper explodes. My list could go on, but I've made my point; there are splintered and fragmented elements of my being. Those expressions of my fractured

3. "Means of Grace."

character need repair. When I observe the means of grace, not only is my spirit made stronger, but my areas of brokenness also begin to mend. The source of that renewal is our God of mercy, the instrument of that healing is my observation of the means of grace.

Do I wish I didn't have my flaws and defects? Sometimes, yes. But I've come to believe that you cannot understand God's grace until you've needed His grace and you can't enjoy God's grace until you've accepted His grace. Well, I've needed His grace a lot! Rest assured, as you place your trust in Him, the healing power of His grace will thrive and so will you!

> *One new perception, one fresh thought, one act of surrender, one change of heart, one leap of faith, can change your life forever.*—Robert Holden

A word of encouragement: we were designed to glorify God and enjoy Him forever. We were given the gifts, talents, and passions we have for a reason — to build up the Kingdom of Heaven and to celebrate every step that brings that vision to life.

In my role as a high school principal, I often met with students. One of my favorite questions to ask them was "Where do you see yourself in 5 or 10 years?" Many times the answer was, "I just want to be happy."

I think if we interviewed adults, a good number of them might answer in much the same way. But here's the thing. When you make happiness your goal, it is always just out of reach. Just around the corner. "I'll be happy when I get this new job. I'll be happy when I get the new car that I've had my eye on. I'll be happy when I buy that house. I'll be happy when. . ." However, we can never quite catch up with happiness or when we do, after the initial excitement, we often feel a little let down. Disappointed.

But joy, true joy, is different. When we fix our eyes on the Kingdom of God, when we begin using our gifts to heal the world, when we begin to love others as we would want to be loved, joy kind of sneaks up from behind and finds us. Joy isn't a short-term high; it is a state of being that we find ourselves in when we ". . .*seek first the kingdom of God*" -Matthew 6:33

If you've gotten this far, you may be wondering, "Where is the single unifying principle for all of life that you promised to reveal in this book?"

Well, buckle up, here we go.

TEN TO ONE

Many people, religious or not, are familiar with the Ten Commandments. These commandments are recorded in the Bible, in the book of Exodus. The context or backstory is that the Jews, or the children of Israel as they are also known, had just been delivered from 400 years of captivity in Egypt. Having been captives and slaves for more than ten generations, they needed guidelines for how to conduct their lives now that they were a free people.

While in captivity, their daily schedules, type of work, even some customs and diet, were prescribed for them by those who had enslaved them, i.e., the Egyptians. Once they were free and on their own, they needed structure to help guide their lives. They needed direction on how they were to live in community together.

You and I need much the same thing while we are in school, at work, or in a community. Even condominium residents have HOA guidelines to adhere to. Unless we live alone on a deserted island, we all need to agree to a code by which to live and interact. I call it a baseline of civilized behavior.

THE BASELINE

The Ten Commandments seem to be very specific. Do this, don't do that. It reminds me of having to be very clear, very specific, with my own children when they were growing up. I even found myself saying things to them that my dad said to me (which I swore I would never say to my kids!)

"Have I communicated clearly?"

"I want the whole truth, the first time I ask, every time I ask."

"Son, in life you are never static; you are moving forward or moving backwards, so do something. Make a decision and move."

And finally, one I borrowed from Paul Newman in *Cool Hand Luke*:

"What we have here is a failure to communicate."[4]

Yes, they would often roll their eyes, letting me know that they had heard these things many times before, but eventually, we learned to communicate, anticipate, analyze, and apply. But there is a progression in our communication with our kids and within our families. The advancement is a natural result of both maturity and trust. As we mature and learn that we are loved and valued, the pin-point precision of specific directives gives way to independent decision-making, thoughtful planning, and empathetic response. In my family, it is usually two steps forward and one step back, but there is a steady movement toward mature and independent thought and action.

Now my children are adults with kids of their own, so we have a very different relationship. I am free to love them, offer help or advice when requested, and to delight in my grandkids.

I believe that we see the same thing occurring in God's commandments to the Israelites. Throughout the five books of the law (the Pentateuch or the Books of Moses), we see a stage-by-stage maturing process: from an emphasis on the specific instruction, rote memorization, and blind obedience needed for toddlers and adolescents, to a mature value system and the acceptance of greater responsibility based on a maturing understanding of the world.

If you've raised kids, you know that you have to be very specific with preschoolers and elementary-aged students and a little less so with middle-schoolers. With teenagers in high school, we just try to keep them on the rails with a combination of logic, reason, a biblical value system, and a healthy fear of Dad and his homicidal tendencies!

How much input do you, or should you have, in helping your kids live happy, healthy, productive lives after college? By the time they graduate from college, our opportunity to insist on certain

4. Rosenberg, *Cool Hand Luke*.

standards of behavior has largely expired. We shouldn't lay down mandates for our children once they are adults and functioning on their own.

But here is the thing. The children of Israel were spiritual infants when they left Egypt, and they needed specific instruction. The remainder of the Old Testament is a collection of stories and poems that illustrate the lessons that God wanted them (and us) to learn. They, too, gradually moved toward a fuller understanding of who God was and how He impacted their daily lives.

I don't know about you, but my life often parallels the children of Israel as they muddled about in the wilderness for 40 years. Some days I get it and feel close to God and am grateful for His intervention on my behalf, and sometimes I fall away and forget how much I am loved. It is often more comfortable to follow rites and rituals than to exercise personal spiritual intuition and the leading of the Holy Spirit.

Entering into an adult relationship with God can be scary!

How much easier it is to default to a list of do's and don'ts than to constantly seek the companionship, love, and direction of God through the Holy Spirit? The Spirit of God defies measurement, is impossible to quantify, and often difficult to predict.

Keeping a healthy relationship with another human being that you can see, touch, feel, and hear is HARD. But how much more attentive and intentional do we have to be to live in fellowship with a person that we can't see? A person who is always there, but whom you have to stop and rest and be quiet to hear? According to the Psalmist in chapter 46 we are instructed to:

"Be still and know that I am God."

Be still?

I'd rather work hard to move toward a measurable goal. Give me some monumental task to complete that will qualify me for a front row seat from which to watch God. Assign me a clear path of difficult but attainable tasks so I can measure my success.

But be still?

I'm no good at that.

Be still?

Rest?

Relax?

Listen instead of talk?

"Be" instead of "Do?"

That is really hard for me.

Under the law of God in the Old Testament, there were lists of good things to do and bad things to avoid. You could see them and measure your relative success or failure in relation to keeping the directives, although we eventually figure out that we can't keep even the simplest of them.

But Jesus comes along and changes the whole deal:

> "Don't misunderstand why I have come—it isn't to cancel the laws of Moses and the warnings of the prophets. No, I came to fulfill them and to make them all come true."
> Matthew 5:17 TLB

Yes, Jesus summarized and restated God's directions for mankind, but He did a lot more than that. Jesus introduced a whole new era and explained our lives in a whole new way. He helped all of those who would listen to enjoy a life of love, freedom, gratitude, and realized destiny.

The religious elite of Jesus' day sought to discredit Him by asking a question that they thought would trip Him up:

> "Teacher, which is the greatest commandment?"

Jesus didn't fall into their trap. They had set the question up so that whatever answer He gave, if He answered as they expected, they could accuse Him of violating the law of God or of blasphemy.

So, what did He do?

He answered their question.

But He answered their question on His terms, not theirs. He made a conscious decision not to be baited into taking a position that would reflect poorly on His father or misrepresent the truth that He came to make our burden light and our yoke easy.

He did not get super-philosophical to talk in circles around them.

He didn't ignore them.

If you read the exchange between Jesus and the Pharisees, you will find that Jesus boiled down the Ten Commandments (and all of the other Old Testament instructions, obligations, stories, poems, mandates, and rituals) into two, easy to remember, impossible to distort, guidelines:

- Love God with all of your heart.
- Love your neighbor as yourself.

Take a look at Jesus' summary and reflect on what His primary intent was as He restated what God requires.

Love God. Love your neighbor.

What would you say if I told you that all of the commandments come down to choosing to live a life that is toxic or a life that is tranquil? What kind of life is tranquil? One full of joy, love, peace, rest, fulfillment, purpose, and promise.

Jesus offers us this "too good to be true" life now.

Let's put the Ten Commandments and words of Jesus into everyday language:

Commandments one through five come down to living our lives from a place of love, gratitude, and rest;

Commandments 1,2 and 3: No God but the one who saved you. God prefaced commandment number one with, *"I am the Lord God that delivered you from slavery."* His primary audience at the time knew very well the hardships and cruelty of slavery. Honoring the God who delivered them from tyranny, brutal labor, and humiliating servitude should have come naturally, an out-working of gratitude.

Commandment 4: A day of rest and celebration. Notice, he commanded them to rest! Remember the Sabbath! Use the day to rest, reflect on the goodness of God, and share that celebration with other believers. What a great way to end the week!

Commandment 5: A heart of gratitude. He reminds us to give honor where honor is due—Mom and Dad. They sacrificed for you, cared for you, put their dreams on hold to help you realize your own. Mom and Dad offered support to help you realize a healthy, happy, abundant life so, "honor your father and mother" is not an unreasonable expectation.

If you weren't parented well, that doesn't mean you can't be a good parent yourself. As you accept the unconditional love and grace of your heavenly Father, you can count on the Holy Spirit to help you make sense of the mistakes your parents made. The chances are good that they had parents who made mistakes too.

As for commandments 6 through 10—the "negative" commandments or the "DO NOT" directives—they boil down to a very simple formula:

Don't want what you don't have.

Don't obsess over getting what someone else owns that you do not.

Commandment 6: Don't kill.

Commandment 7: Don't take someone else's wife.

Commandment 8: Don't steal.

Commandment 9: Don't lie.

Commandment 10: Don't imagine ways to take what your friends or neighbors have.

What does 6+7+8+9+10 equal?

Be content.

Enjoy what you have.

Trust God to meet your needs. Loving God boils down to expressing love and living in joy. Delighting that our God loves us enough to pursue us. Living in a way that shows honor, an honor inspired by the awe-inspiring acts of love He demonstrates on our behalf.

We have now set the stage for the single unifying principle for all of life that I promised at the beginning of this book.

We have the ten "commandments" to help us understand how we can live in harmony with others. Jesus then summarizes those precepts into two main ideas: "*Love God with all of your heart and your neighbor as yourself*" Matthew 22:37.

And finally, Jesus brings us back to a single idea or principle that we can use as a compass to guide our lives. It is found in his Sermon on the Mount.

"Seek ye first the Kingdom of God and His righteousness and all these things will be added unto you."—Matthew 6:33 KJV

Be concerned about God's kingdom and His way of doing things and everything else you need will be provided for you. There you have it— one single, unifying principle for all of life. Simple. Not easy. But hard to misunderstand. Seek God and His kingdom above all else and you will have everything you need.

DIVINE GUARANTEE

We've all heard of the "Lifetime Guarantee" for various products, but what about an eternal guarantee, one that will never expire? Well, now you have one. Not only are you redeemed, as a son or daughter of God, you are also an heir of heaven and its goodness. God has put down a security deposit to establish that you are a beneficiary both now, in this life, and in the future. So, while the world sees and understands the concept of passing from life to death, we, as beloved members of the family of God, pass from death to life.

"Truly, truly, I say to you, whoever hears my word and believes him who sent me has eternal life. He does not come into judgment but has passed from death to life." -John 5:24 ESV

When it comes to finalizing the estate of someone who has passed away, final wills and documents are reviewed, signed, sealed, and protected to ensure that there are no misunderstandings. If there is any challenge to your status as a beneficiary, the records are available when needed. If someone tries to remove you from your place as a beneficiary, you may stop those efforts by producing the estate and trust documents.

As a believer, you will find the trust documents in Ephesians:

"And you also were included in Christ when you heard the message of truth, the gospel of your salvation. When you believed, you were marked in him with a seal, the promised Holy Spirit, who is a deposit guaranteeing our inheritance

until the redemption of those who are God's possession, to the praise of his glory." -Ephesians 1:13–14 NIV

In His goodness, God not only provided our restoration to His family, but He also put up a security deposit to finalize and establish our status as His children. This status is now irrevocable.

And just what is the security or earnest deposit that God put up to finalize our adoption and inheritance? Our guarantee is the Holy Spirit of God who takes up residence within us. He brings with Him an inward heaven to be a part of us while we wait for the complete joys of our eternal heaven. That promised land will include a perfect and sinless personal condition as well as a fully restored place at the family table of our Father.

The result of our guarantee?

Peace. Rest. Joy.

> *"Peace I leave with you; my peace I give you. I do not give to you as the world gives. Do not let your hearts be troubled, and do not be afraid."*—John 14:27 NIV

You may rest knowing that Jesus has promised to meet all of your needs and that He has sent to us the Holy Spirit as the first installment of that provision.

How will He supply in your situation?

Individually.

Your story is a unique, one-of-a-kind adventure designed specifically for you.

No two diamonds are alike. They differ in size, cut, clarity and color and thus are identifiable as individual gems. Similarly, your life is particular, set apart, and unique. All the twists and turns, challenges, obstacles, and victories are yours for the living. God will work in your life in a manner that fits perfectly for you.

I can testify to this. For more than 50 years, God has met every single one of my needs. Unfortunately, sometimes I recognize His hand in the provision, and sometimes I chalk it up to my hard work and fail to recognize that "*every good and perfect gift is from above coming from the Father.*" But I can assure you that if you let Him, He will meet all of your needs as well.

*"God is never late and rarely early. He is always exactly right on time—His time." -*Dillon Burroughs[5]

Now what?

"So do not fear, for I am with you;
do not be dismayed, for I am your God.
I will strengthen you and help you;
I will uphold you with my righteous right hand."
-Isaiah: 41:10 NIV

I am sure of this. I have newfound freedom that I can only attribute to accepting and trusting in my identity as a child of God and an heir of Heaven. Part of this liberation is that I no longer feel obligated to be a "striver" to achieve specific goals. I no longer have to overcome obstacles and hardships to prove who I am. Being freed from the need to "strive," I feel joy and freedom that I have not felt before. I have the freedom to thrive instead of strive.

Suddenly I am at peace. I am free to enjoy life and who I am, and I feel that I can walk in this freedom forever. I pray that you, too, will find the peace of God that passes all understanding.

5. Burroughs, "God Is Never Late."

A Final Word

THE TRUTH OF THE world we live in is this—it was created by a visionary, artistic God who envisioned and conceived a vibrant, productive, loving, caring, beautiful, magnificent world full of men and women who, out of the free-will delegated to them, come to know a personal God and in so doing bring to life an original work of art in its perfect form. A masterpiece that He contemplated, envisioned and initiated, that started with Adam. It was this same loving creator who delegated to mankind the gift of a free will. Although we have experienced the trauma and tragedy of the fall, by His redemption and rescue we are the evidence of a work perfected, to give us a vested interest and ownership in creation.

What tremendous power lies in living without fear and walking in faith. When once our principles and goals are aligned with those of the author of the universe, a confidence of thought and action is born. No longer weighed down by guilt and a fear of failure, our minds and souls are free to be about the work of the King and His kingdom.

Make no mistake, we are not only talking about a heavenly kingdom or a life after death kingdom—we are talking about the here and now business of the King of all the universe. We are talking about boldly going out to do justice and mercy, knowing that the one who has called us will also supply us with all necessary resources and connections.

The mind of a man in the hands of God has the power to heal the sick or move a mountain.

The soul of a man shaped by the heart of God speaks hope to the hopeless, power to the powerless and echoes love down the long halls of eternity.

A man whose mind and soul move in concert with the eternal, omnipotent, magnificent Spirit of God become the hands and feet of Jesus and an irresistible force that can move mountains, part a raging sea, bind up the wounds of the broken, defend the weak, feed the hungry, clothe the naked, turn water into wine, and heal the world!

God only knows what things we can accomplish when we are empowered by his grace and fueled by his love. It is now up to you and me to decide; will we bury ourselves in the day-to-day concerns of this world, or will we live in the truth that we are wonderfully created, deeply loved and destined for glory?

The choice is yours.

I say, choose love, my friend.

Seek ye first the Kingdom of God and His righteousness and all these things will be added unto you!!—Jesus

Bibliography

Burroughs, Dillon. "God Is Never Late and Rarely Early. He Is Always Exactly Right On Time—His Time." Used by permission. https://www.goodreads. com/quotes/789710-god-is-never-late-and-rarely-early-he-is-always.

Carr, Flora. "The Real Reason Why Mary Magdalene Is Such a Controversial Figure." *Time*, Mar 30, 2018. https://time.com/5210705/mary-magdalene-controversial/.

Elliot, Jim. *The Journals of Jim Elliot*. Fleming H. Revell Company, 1978.

Henley, William Ernest. "Invictus." Poetry Foundation, 1875. https://www.poetry foundation.org/poems/51642/invictus.

Holden, Robert. *Shift Happens!: Powerful Ways to Transform Your Life*. UNKNO, 2006.

Hugo, Victor. *Les Miserables*. Enriched Classics. International Collectors Library, 1964.

Keller, Tim. *The King's Cross: The Story of the World in the Life of Jesus*. New York: Dutton, 2011.

King, Martin Luther, Jr. "I Have a Dream Speech."

Krohn, Paysach J. *Perfection at the Plate: Echoes of the Maggid*. Mesorah Publications, 1999.

Lao Tzu. "Chapter 64." In *Tao Te Ching*. Harper Perennial, 1900.

Manning, Brennan. *The Ragamuffin Gospel*. Multnomah, 1990.

———. *The Wisdom of Tenderness*. San Francisco: HarperOne, 2004. Reprint ed.

Manning, Brennan, and John Blasé. *All Is Grace: A Ragamuffin Memoir*. David C Cook, 2011.

"Means of Grace." Ligonier Ministries, Jun 26, 2012. https://www.ligonier.org/learn/devotionals/means-of-grace.

Miller, Ashley. "Shoes for the Race." https://ashleymiller.theworldrace.org/post/radical-living.

Rosenberg, Stuart, dir. *Cool Hand Luke*. Jalem Productions, 1967.

Sophocles. *Antigone*. New York: Dover, 1993.

Taylor, Anne. "Man Showed Love for His Neighbor during Dark Days." Interfaith Movement, Jul 14, 2018. https://interfaithmovement.com/news/man-show ed-love-for-his-neighbor-during-dark-days/.

Bibliography

ten Boom, Corrie. *Tramp for the Lord*. USA: CLC Publications, 2008.

"Wrunken the Martyr." Percykids' Weblog, Feb 23, 2020. https://percykids.wordpress.com/2020/02/23/wrunken-the-martyr/.

Wylie, James Aitken. *The History of Protestantism*. Vol. 1. London, Paris, New York: Cassell and Company. https://www.doctrine.org/history/HPv1b5.htm.

Wytsma, Ken. *Pursuing Justice: The Call to Live and Die for Bigger Things*. Thomas Nelson, 2013.

www.ingramcontent.com/pod-product-compliance
Lightning Source LLC
Chambersburg PA
CBHW060312100426

42812CB00003B/750